AF521857

# FIELDER'S HERBAL HELPER

# FIELDER'S HERBAL HELPER

# OR HUNTERS, TRAPPERS, AND FISHERMEN

## MILDRED FIELDER

WINCHESTER PRESS • TULSA, OKLAHOMA

*To those who like to breathe the clean, clear air of the mountains, to see the sparkle of the tumbling brooks and streams, to hear the crackle of the autumn leaves as they walk through the woods, who remember that there was a time when hunting and fishing were the only ways to put meat on the dinner table.*

*They will understand why wild plant lures were considered seriously, and will perhaps consider them so again.*



*Quotations from the works of J. B. Wyeth, H. H. Brackenridge, and John Bradbury are used with the permission of the publisher of* Early Western Travels, *edited by Reuben G. Thwaites, The Arthur H. Clark, Co., Glendale, California.*

*Library of Congress Cataloging in Publication Data*

*Fielder, Mildred.*
*Fielder's herbal helper for hunters, trappers, and fishermen.*
*Bibliography: p.*
*Includes index.*
*1. Hunting—North America—Folklore. 2. Trapping—North America—Folklore. 3. Fishing—North America—Folklore. 4. Plants—North America—Folklore. 5. Plants, Useful—North America—Identification. I. Title.*
*GR101.F53 398'.368 81-21821*
*ISBN 0-87691-361-3 AACR2*

*Published by Winchester Press*
*1421 South Sheridan Road*
*P. O. Box 1260*
*Tulsa, Oklahoma 74101*

*A Talisman/Winchester book*

*Designed by Nancy Etheredge*

*Printed in the United States of America*

*1 2 3 4 5 86 85 84 83 82*

# CONTENTS

# ACKNOWLEDGMENTS

To the members of the Homestake Library, Lead, S.D., and to members of the San Luis Obispo City Public Library in San Luis Obispo and Los Osos, Calif., my thanks for special help in securing source material.

Research materials were acquired through the library bibliographical centers from the following sources: South Dakota Free Library Commission, Pierre, S.D.; University of Denver, Denver, Colo.; Deadwood City Library, Deadwood, S.D.; University of Wyoming, Laramie, Wy.; Missouri Historical Society, St. Louis, Mo.; Denver Public Library, Denver, Colo.; University of Michigan, Ann Arbor, Mich.; University of North Dakota, Grand Forks, N.D.; University of Colorado, Boulder, Colo.; Wisconsin Historical Society; South Dakota Historical Society, Pierre, S.D.; and Milwaukee Public Museum, Milwaukee, Wisc.

To Alice and Henry Meyer, my thanks for their help in identifying many of the California plants.

To Robert Elman, my grateful appreciation for his generosity in sharing his knowledge of fishing and hunting lore.

Though all of the books listed in the bibliography were useful at one time or another in compiling this book, I am particularly indebted to the reports of Melvin R. Gilmore and to his research on the plants used by the Indians of the Missouri River basin, to Huron H. Smith for his writings on the Indians of Wisconsin, and to the several California botanical handbooks listed in the bibliography.

My special thanks to the following individuals, publishers, and agencies for their help in obtaining and their permission to reproduce many of the photographs in this book: California Department of Agriculture; County of Los Angeles, Department of Arboreta and Botanic Gardens; Doubleday & Company, Inc.; Dover Publications, Inc.; Robert

Fielder; Maxine Fielder; Kate Jones; Loomis Museum Association, Volcanic National Park; Henry W. Meyer; Majorie Marcom; U.S. Department of Agriculture; U.S. Department of the Interior; U.S. Forest Service; U.S. Soil Conservation Service; University of South Dakota Museum; Della B. Vik; Dirk R. Walters; and Winchester Press.

Acknowledgment is also extended to the publishers of the following magazines, in which I have previously published articles directly or indirectly concerned with subjects discussed in this book: *Canadian Red Cross, Jr.; Dakota Farmer; Denver Post Empire Magazine; Discovery for Juniors; Junior Discoveries; National Parks and Conservation Magazine; Nature; New England Homestead; Snowy Egret; Trout; Venture.*

# PREFACE

Wild plants were once thought to be very beneficial to the hunter and the fisherman, and to help the horses that carried sportsmen to their destinations. Though the benefits of these plants may be only superstitions, today our renewed interest in the environment suggests that we should at least recognize the existence of these old-time hunting and fishing baits, lures, and aids. If in the process of reading about them you are also entertained, so much the better.

As an authority for scientific botanical names, I have referred to *Standardized Plant Names*, by Harlan P. Kelsey and William A. Dayton. Photo identification has been aided primarily by the excellent descriptions and illustrations in Henry A. Gleason's *The New Britton and Brown Illustrated Flora of the United States and Canada*, but many other references were also consulted. In some cases, when photographs of the plants discussed were not available, photographs of closely related species were used as illustrations. Wherever such substitutions occur, an effort is made to differentiate the two species for identification purposes.

Since this is a folklore book written for its historical and entertainment value, I have included many popular or familiar names for the various plants. While Britton's and Brown's *Illustrated Flora of the Northern United States, Canada and the British Possessions* was of great help in assigning common names, other historical and botanical sources were of value as well.

The common names of wild plants overlap with such consistent inconsistency that we must fall back on the botanical names for final identification. Those who want to find these plants are urged to do so by checking all available reference sources pertaining to the one you may be searching for to get the whole picture. Lists of common names for each plant are not always repeated, usually being included only once. If you know a familiar name for the plant in question, by following through on all references to its Latin name, obtained by trial and error reference, you can ultimately find the full information you may want.

Several states have lists of protected plants that may not be picked or otherwise endangered; this information is generally available through state arboretums or natural history departments. I urge those interested in historical plants to exercise particular care for these rare species, so that they will survive to delight and instruct the generations that follow us.

MILDRED FIELDER
*Los Osos, Calif.*
*May 1980*

# SECTION 1

# PREPARE YOURSELF

Hunting or fishing is not a game for an out-of-shape person, man or woman. You have to be fairly fit to hold that gun steady, and you must keep healthy during the season.

The subject of wild plant medicine is a broad one, going back to the distant times when the only medicines known were the witches' brews or the magic of the medicine man. Archaeologists have found that even the earliest man had his infections and tumors, and that he tried to cure them with what was at hand.

Herbs, massage, poultices, and special diets all entered into those primitive cures. There is evidence that in extreme cases of illness the patient was even killed to rid the group of the burden of caring for him. Medicine men leaned heavily on the power of suggestion in their magic rites and incantations, but even back then they at times depended on chemical reaction from certain plants.

This is not a book on medicine. It is a lighthearted look at hunting and fishing as it once was, and as it could be again.

To this end, I will begin with a few suggestions on how a hunter or fisherman in the woods can protect his body from the onslaughts of insects, sharpen his senses with certain elixirs, and even give himself a lift from a brew such as the Old Woodsman's Liquor Formula.

Only then is he really ready to pursue his chosen quarry.

# 1.

# SUBDUE THOSE INSECTS

Hunting is such a good sport that even if you are allergic to insect bites of one kind or another it is worth knowing some of the things you can do about them, so that you can continue to follow game even in the buggiest marsh or forest.

The intrepid explorers of western America met mosquitoes in such hordes that the buzzing clouds should have quailed the strongest heart. They found the insects hovering in the river valleys so thickly that during calm weather it was nearly impossible to leave their tents or boats. John Wyeth wrote in 1833, "At this point of our journey we were sadly tormented by musquetoes [*sic*] that prevented our sleep after the fatigues of the day. This little contemptible insect which they call here a gnat, disturbed us more than bears, or wolves, or snakes."[1]

Of course there were bees, wasps, ticks, and other varmints of like nature, too. There were also spider bites to contend with; woodsmen treated these with yarrow leaves.

*Achillea lanulosa*, western yarrow or woolly yarrow.

*Achillea millefolium*, common yarrow.

These two yarrows are so much alike in appearance that they can easily be mistaken for each other, yet I find mention of only the western yarrow (also called woolly yarrow) as a poultice for spider bite. The finely dissected leaves are crushed together and placed over the spider bite to draw out any possible poison in the flesh.

1. Wyeth, J. B., *Oregon: or a Short History of a Long Journey from the Atlantic Ocean to the Region of the Pacific*, p. 56.

*Achillea millefolium,* common yarrow.

Both yarrows grow from one to three feet high, depending on soil and climate conditions. Their leaves are like little green feathers sprouting opposite each other in very slender and crowded divisions. The flower heads are usually flat-topped, but they may be slightly domed. As far as I can tell, the main difference between the two is the color of the flower heads. Both species carry white flowers, but the *Achillea millefolium* may show tinges of rose, and the *Achillea lanulosa* may be yellowish as well as white.

The yellowish yarrow, *A. lanulosa,* was well known in the swamplands of Virginia as a toothache treatment, so it must grow in eastern states as well as in western regions. Chew the leaves. Make a poultice of those small leaves and you have something to heal inflammation, to stop bleeding in wounds, or to heal a rash.

Smoke the flower heads with other plants for ceremonial purposes. Mix the flower heads and the leaves together, simmer them to make a medicinal brew, and you have a mild laxative, a tonic, and a help for indigestion or a generally rundown condition. White settlers thought it cured menstrual problems or any ailment in the gastrointestinal tract or the reproductive organs.

*Achillea lanulosa* is also called wild tansy when the blossoms show yellow.

*Artemisia ludoviciana*, Louisiana sagebrush. (Photo by Karl E. Graetz. Courtesy of U.S. Department of Agriculture, Soil Conservation Service.)

*Artemisia vulgaris heterophylla*, California mugwort. (Photo from *Weeds of California*, by W.W. Robbins, Margaret K. Bellue, and Walter S. Ball. Courtesy of California Department of Agriculture.) ▶

The common yarrow, *A. millefolium*, so nearly like the western yarrow, had the same powers and a few others. The Scots believed it was an effective love charm if put under the loved one's pillow at night. Moisten a wad of leaves with yarrow infusion, then place that wad in your ear to get rid of an earache. Cures for colds, fever, swellings — a mighty power is wielded by the modest yarrow.

The common yarrow is so widely found that it has acquired a bundle of names. You may know it as one of these: milfoil, millefolium, thousand-leaf, thousand-leaf clover, gordoloba, green arrow, soldiers' woundwort, nosebleed, dog daisy, bloodwort, sanquinary, carpenter grass, old man's pepper, cammock, or ladies' mantle.

## *Artemisia ludoviciana*, Louisiana sagebrush.

## *Artemisia vulgaris heterophylla*, California mugwort.

The leaves of Louisiana sagebrush, also known as white sage, western mugwort, lobed cudweed or sagebrush, were smoked in a campfire as a particularly good smudge to drive away mosquitoes. Almost any kind of smoke can be used as a smudge if the mosquitoes are bothering you too much in the evening's twilight, but if the Louisiana sagebrush is more effective we might as well know it. That same smudge cured a horse's distemper, so there must be some chemical medicine in those leaves.

The name Louisiana sagebrush was coined because the plant grows near St. Louis, Missouri, although it is also found in Utah, Texas, and Arizona.

A poultice was made of the leaves and used to treat sores of long standing. Steep the leaves and you have a tea for tonsillitis or sore throat. White settlers made a brew from the white sage for digestive ills or ailments in the genital tracts. When mountain men roamed alone in unexplored lands they sometimes contracted a sickness that they called mountain fever, and this malady was also treated by a tea made from the Louisiana sagebrush.

Sioux Indians along the Missouri River added it to other leaves to make a smoking tobacco, but I am not sure which mixture contained it. The prairie Indians had several blends of wild plants to smoke in their pipes.

Louisiana sagebrush or western mugwort may share a valuable trait with the California mugwort, *Artemisia vulgaris heterophylla*, which translates to "mixleaf mugwort wormwood," so named because of the variety of shapes seen in its leaves. It is said that if you get poison oak rash on the West Coast (and poison oak is prolific in that area), you can rub mugwort leaves on the rash and it will be cured. If Louisiana sagebrush has the same effect, it is a good plant to know for more than simply smoking out mosquitoes.

## *Chrysanthemum parthenium*, feverfew chrysanthemum.

People who are allergic to bees know that a bee sting is no joke. You can carry a bee-sting kit with you, but in case you do not have access to such a kit, the feverfew chrysanthemum will help you avoid the bees.

Once the feverfew blooms, its white flower rays last a long time on the stalks, thus making the plant easier to spot. Carry a handful of those flower heads in your pocket or rub them over exposed parts of your body like hands, face, neck — and ankles if you are not wearing boots. Bees just don't like the smell of the flowers and will leave you alone.

The feverfew has many other values. Among them is that it will make a beverage for you to take if you catch cold in the woods. Brew the flowers and some of the leaves together, and drink the result. The warm infusion will attack a cold; it will also help if you have gas on the stomach. If there is any left after drinking the warm brew, keep it. Cold, the extract is still good as a tonic. The virtues of the plant will be intensified if it is steeped for a while in alcohol instead of water, but water works well, too.

To make the brew, steep a heaping teaspoon of bits of the flowers and leaves per cup of boiling water according to quantities needed, for half an hour. Drink one or two cups of this a day — warm for a cold or for gas pains, cold for a general tonic.

Besides being a good tonic, the brew will relieve colic or other forms of gas cramps, help menstrual problems, get rid of worms in the body, and produce a temporary increase of vitality. The fact that it has a strong, unpleasant smell and a bitter taste probably encouraged the early Americans to treat it as a medicine, but if bees and wasps will also avoid it, that is one good point for even the healthiest hunter to remember.

Also known as febrifuge plant, *Chrysanthemum parthenium* is an erect, bushy herb growing from one to two and a half feet tall. The leaves are sometimes as long as six inches, thin and hairy. They appear alternately on the stalk, the lower ones growing on stems and the upper ones growing directly from the stalk. They are pinnately parted, and each segment is toothed as well. *C. parthenium* is closely related to the oxeye daisy, *C. leucanthemum*, known all over America. The main difference is that the oxeye daisy has one blossom at the top of its stem and the feverfew has a loose group of smaller white-rayed heads.

## *Datura stramonium*, jimsonweed.

The jimsonweed is one of the most dangerous plants you can fool with, yet old wives' tales in the southern states insist that a jimson-

*Chrysanthemum leucanthemum*, oxeye daisy.

weed leaf placed on mosquito bites will take the sting and swelling away quickly. That leaf was also poulticed against infected wounds or any skin wound; it was believed to lower fevers if the leaf poultice was applied somewhere on the body.

These beliefs may be true, but the entire plant is dangerously poisonous and narcotic. It is found east and west across America. I have photographed jimsonweed in North Carolina, and in California. Surely it is beautiful with its large white funnel-shaped flowers up to eight inches long, the white of the flowers sometimes tinged with lavender. Even its thorny seed vessels are interesting, but the plant stinks like mad. That stink is the only virtue I can give it. If its putrid smell will make you leave it alone, it has served a good purpose.

The leaves and seeds have been used medically, but the jimsonweed's primary action is to cause severe hallucinations. Too big a dose will kill you. The name was derived from the name of Jamestown, Virginia, where an attempt was made in 1675 to overthrow the governor. The conditions among the insurgents went from bad to worse, and when the hungry soldiers nibbled on some of the seeds of *Datura stramonium*, they were delirious for days, completely out of their minds, sick with nausea, vomiting, and convulsions, even sinking into comas.

In spite of its evil effects, priests once gave the powdered root to members of their tribes to induce sleep and to help them see ghosts. They probably saw more than ghosts, but hallucinatory drugs have been part of religions in various primitive societies.

More recently it has been claimed that if leaves are dried completely, then crumbled like tobacco, smoking of the dried leaves in a pipe will give relief to asthmatic victims. I do not vouch for this. I wouldn't touch the stuff.

Jimsonweed has many names, and I am sure you can guess how some of them originated. Know it as datura, thorn-apple, Jamestown weed, Jamestown lily, devil's apple, madapple, stinkweed, stinkwort, devil's trumpet, fireweed, dewtry, apple of Peru, Jamestown oak, tolquacha, or angel tulip.

### *Hamamelis virginiana*, witch hazel.

Witch-hazel lotion has long been known as a good soothing agent for mosquito bites. The plant is a tall shrub fond of damp woods; mosquitoes like damp woods, too, so the two are often found together.

The branches and twigs should be cut in the late autumn or early winter months. Place them in a pot and cover them with water. Simmer them slowly for an hour or more until you are sure the oil has permeated the water. Remove from the fire and cool. This solution can

*Datura stramonium*, jimsonweed.

*Hamamelis virginiana*, witch hazel. (Photo by Dirk R. Walters.)

be rubbed on mosquito bites or aching muscles as it is, but if you add alcohol to the mixture you will get better results.

The witch hazel is a strange tree. It flowers in the fall, not the spring, waiting until the leaves are ready to fall before making even an attempt to flower. Then you will see its tiny yellow strings of flowers dangling from the twigs in a cloud of color. Seed pods develop from the flowers. When the pods are ripe they open to release two little black seeds shaped like footballs.

You can eat those seeds if you want, as they are quite safe. For primitive Indian tribes in what is now Wisconsin the seeds were part of a sacred medicine ceremony.

Witch-hazel lotion has been known for centuries and has long been a popular rubbing lotion used by athletes to keep their muscles limber. Lame backs, swellings, skin tumors, all have been treated with the lotion.

The dried leaves of witch hazel are listed in a twentieth-century pharmaceutical handbook as an astringent or an agent to control bleeding, but an added notation indicates that "its virtues have been greatly exaggerated."[2] Maybe so. But witch-hazel lotion is a distillation of

2. Remington, Joseph P., *The Practice of Pharmacy*, p. 1301.

the oil, not the leaves alone, so who knows? You can purchase it today, and plenty of people do.

The plant has other names: snapping hazel, winterbloom, wych-hazel, striped alder, spotted alder, and tobacco wood.

## *Hedeoma pulegioides*, American falsepennyroyal.

The American falsepennyroyal, known much more familiarly as simply pennyroyal or American pennyroyal, also has the common names of mosquito plant and tickweed, as well as mock pennyroyal, squawmint, stinking balm, and hedeoma. Notice the names mosquito plant and tickweed especially. The fragrance of the plant is strong enough, pungent and aromatic, that it is obnoxious to fleas, mosquitoes, and ticks. This can be a true boon to the woodsman.

Gather a few leaves and tie them securely to your dog's collar—no fleas or ticks. Rub a few leaves on your hands, your neck, your arms, or any part of your skin exposed to the air, and you will discourage the mosquitoes as well as the fleas that might attack you and your dog. Wood ticks are not welcome visitors either, so anything that will repel them is an extra bonus.

The authors of *Standardized Plant Names*, Harlan Kelsey and William A. Dayton, call *Hedeoma pulegioides* American falsepennyroyal instead of the simpler American pennyroyal, and they do this for a reason. In England and other parts of Europe, long before the colonists came to America, pennyroyal existed (and still exists) as a wild plant, but it was *Mentha pulegium* or *Mentha pulegioides*, and not *Hedeoma pulegioides*. Both of these European pennyroyals are members of the mint family. Both are much alike but have minor differences. Both have the pungent minty scent and taste, but only in Europe does the *Mentha pulegium* grow; and only in America does the *Hedeoma pulegioides* grow. In spite of all this, most American botanists drop the word false and refer to the *Hedeoma* spp.[3] as pennyroyal without apology to anyone. So call it pennyroyal if you want. Others do.

It is a low-growing plant, fairly common. It grows from five to eight or ten inches high, rarely as tall as twelve inches. Its slender, square stem is erect and much branched, somewhat hairy, bearing small, thin, narrow leaves. Those half-inch-long leaves are oblong, growing opposite each other.

The flowers are few and clustered, and what flowers exist are pale

3. The botanists' abbreviations sp. for one species and spp. for more than one species will be used throughout this book.

blue with the corolla scarcely exceeding the calyx beneath the petals. The plant is unimpressive except for that strong scent.

When the pennyroyal is in flower the leaves and flowering tops are collected. A limited industry exists to distill oil from these, and pennyroyal oil or leaves can be purchased in some natural-food stores.

Indians along the Missouri River once distilled a medicine for colds from the leaves. Later sources call pennyroyal tea a sleep inducer. Even as late as 1934 we find references to the proper dosage of pennyroyal tea to promote perspiration when you have a fever, or need a stimulant, or have stomach cramps.

Despite all these suggestions, pennyroyal should be completely ignored as a medicine. Within the past few years the deaths or serious illnesses of women taking pennyroyal oil to induce abortions have been reported by reputable medical sources. Liver complications and diffuse bleeding occurred, blamed strictly on that oil of pennyroyal.

This does not change the fact that the strong scent of the pennyroyal rubbed externally on the skin will repel insects.

## *Plantago major*, rippleseed plantain.

The rippleseed plantain is a small weedy-appearing plant, not very big and not very noticeable, but does it have power!

Make a hot tea from the leaves. Cool it enough that it will not scald the skin, and wash it over a bee sting to take the poison from the flesh. This is supposed to work on snakebites, too, or to soothe burns and scalds. If you don't want to wait for the tea to brew and cool, press the fresh leaves immediately on a bee sting or a mosquito bite as a poultice. It will give fast relief, I am told.

The leaves are oval and ribbed, growing in a circle on the ground from the center root. The narrow spike climbs from the center of the leaves and carries small whitish blooms that get seedy in a hurry. The plants that I have found have never been over ten or twelve inches high at the most, and it is easy to walk past it without seeing it if you are not looking specifically for the plantain.

Its folklore goes back to the Greeks and the Saxons, and its healing qualities are due to the chemistry of the plant. It contains potash, potassium, wax, pectin, and resin, as well as citric and oxalic acids. The potash may well be the healer of human flesh, though the potassium is also essential to good health.

Greeks gathered plantain and used it to heal ulcers and wounds. The Saxons said it was a basic medicine for infectious diseases. The standard remedy for dysentery was said to be three handfuls of roots and leaves boiled in a pint of water; the resulting brew was drunk by the sick person as often as he wanted it.

In America, Iroquois Indians found the leaf poultice valuable in any wounds, for insect stings, sores, rheumatism, and burns and swellings, and they made a leaf brew for coughs, colds, and bronchitis.

Ojibwa Indians believed that if you carried a root of rippleseed plantain you would have a magic charm against snakes. Just carry it, that's all. The snakes will leave you alone.

If the snake ignores the charm and bites you anyway, make that tea from the leaves and wash the snakebite area to cure it. The Iroquois made a leaf poultice of plantain to place over the bite of a rattlesnake or any other snake.

Earache was cured by juice of the leaves, and the root was chewed for toothache.

Thorns and splinters can be extracted from the flesh by heating a plantain leaf and holding it against the splinter. It will come out easily, according to the lore of the Sioux tribes.

What more? That ought to be enough for one small plant, but you can also eat it if you have a mind to.

The plantain has several names, one of which might ring a bell for you if you do not know it as rippleseed plantain. How about common plantain, Indian wheat, greater plantain, dooryard plantain, wayside plantain, roundleaf plantain, broadleaf, henplant, lamb's foot, way bread, or healing blade?

*Plantago major*, rippleseed plantain. (Photo by Marjorie Morcom.)

A recent (1980) statement from Jefferson Medical College, Philadelphia, declares that plantain leaves are an excellent remedy for poison ivy. Crush the leaves and rub them on poison ivy rash; the itching will disappear quickly, and the rash will not spread to other parts of the body.

*Sambucus callicarpa*, Pacific red elderberry.

*Sambucus canadensis*, American elder.

*Sambucus cerulea*, blueberry elder.

Of the several varieties of elderberries, these three with edible berries were particularly favored to treat bee stings, or indeed to keep away any sort of insect. The leaves and flowers of the Pacific red elderberry and the blueberry elder were poulticed on a bee sting to soothe the hurt. The leaves of the American elder were bruised, simmered, then used as a lotion to repel bees and other insects or to cure their bites.

The elderberries are magic, if one can believe old legends. One legend says that the cross of Jesus was constructed from the wood of the elder and that all its marvelous powers stem from the death of Jesus on that cross of elder wood. It was once believed, for instance, that if a person was baptized and his eyes anointed with the green juice of its inner bark, that person could recognize witches whenever he saw them. An elder planted near your home would also keep the evil spirits from your home. Elderberries gathered on St. John's Night were part of a mystic rite to make a person invisible. Moreover, if you were to stand underneath an elder tree during a lightning storm, the lightning would not strike you. All that is legend.

The elders are small trees or shrubs with great clusters of blossoms and berries. Elderberries are rich in vitamin A, calcium, thiamine, niacin, and protein, and so they are a valuable food. Though the shrubs are around five feet tall, some of the species can be thirty-foot trees. The elders grow all across America, up to 9,000 feet in the mountains and at sea level near the oceans.

The opposite leaves are pointed and jagged-edged, with an uneven number of leaflets, from five to eleven on a stem. The big clusters of flowers are sometimes globular, sometimes flat-topped, depending on the species.

The flowers can be added in cooked recipes. The berries are excellent for wines, cordials, jellies, jams, sauces, and even pies.

*Sambucus callicarpa* is the only one of the red elderberry species that I found to be eaten or made into a drink, though it is wise to cook the berries of even this one before eating them. Generally speaking,

*Sambucus callicarpa*, Pacific red elderberry.

*Sambucus canadensis*, American elder.

*Sambucus cerulea*, blueberry elder.

other red elderberries are considered to be inedible or downright poisonous, though this has not been definitely proven.

The leaves and flowers of *S. callicarpa* were steeped for use on bee stings. A black dye was obtained from the bark. The plant has no other common names.

The American elder, *Sambucus canadensis*, is one of the most widespread elders and one of the most popular. Its black or dark blue berries are quite edible, cooked or raw, for jams, pies, wine, in pancake batter, or however you like. The blossoms, when dipped in hot water, made a pleasant beverage, but when dried they were a medicine for fevers and an infusion for use on sores, blisters, and hemorrhoids. An elderberry water was made to induce perspiration in patients with common colds, to take as a gargle, or to soothe inflamed eyes. Some people have also eaten the flowers after dipping them in a batter and frying them.

Purple dye came from the berries, and yellow dye from the buds. The stems were used by small boys to make popguns.

It is known that the fresh leaves, flowers, bark, young buds, and roots contain chemicals that under certain conditions produce prussic acid, and therefore they must be treated with extreme care. Nevertheless, all were used to make medicine at one time. The leaves were bruised and used to keep insects from other plants as well as from man.

The root bark of the American elder was steeped to free lungs of phlegm. The inner bark of the young shoots was known to be a diuretic and a purgative, and a bark tea made from the branch bark was given to a mother when she had a difficult childbirth and the baby was born dead. Chickasaw Indians soaked the branches of the American elder in warm water with some kind of cedar, pounded them, and made a poultice for headaches.

Other common names for *S. canadensis* are black-berried elder, sweet elder, sambucus, elder flowers, elder blows, elder, and black elder.

*Sambucus cerulea*, blueberry elder, produces blue berries, as the name indicates, but they are a much lighter blue than the American elder's berries.

The inner bark of the blueberry elder was steeped to make a tea that was given to one who was sick to the stomach and vomiting. On the other hand, if someone actually ate that inner bark it would cause him to vomit. If you used the inner bark at all, you had to be careful to know what you were doing.

The blue elderberries should not be eaten raw, but if they are cooked they can be eaten in pies, jellies, wine, or whatever you want.

A brew of the dried blossom made a lotion and antiseptic wash and was also taken internally to check bleeding of the lungs in consump-

*Solidago rigida*,
stiff goldenrod.

tion. In California the early Spanish-Americans called the blossoms *sauco* and simmered them for a tea for a bad cold, to cause the patient to sweat.

The hollowed stems made good flutes, and black dye was obtained from the young branches.

Other common names for the blueberry elder are blue elderberry and common elder.

## *Solidago rigida*, stiff goldenrod.

Of the sixty-four species of goldenrod specifically named and recognized, it seems strange that only the stiff goldenrod is mentioned as having a medicinal use, as a lotion to soothe bee stings.

Meskwaki Indians of the midwestern frontier lands simmered the flowers and washed the resulting lotion over a bee sting to draw the poison from the skin. The same flower lotion could be gargled to cure a swollen throat.

The leaves were boiled simply to make a beverage for drinking, though I have no idea what that beverage tasted like.

The stiff goldenrod is a tall, stout plant growing in dry soil, the stalk hoary-downy and rough. The thick oval or oblong leaves have a strong midrib. The yellow-flowered heads are crowded in a large terminal compound corymb, generally flat-topped but often irregular in the shape of the inflorescence.

The stiff goldenrod has one other common name. Some call it hard-leaved goldenrod.

# 2.

# SHARPEN YOUR SENSES

There isn't a hunter alive who doesn't know the amazing ability of an animal to camouflage itself, to blend with its background. If it stands still, and it will if it is frightened, you cannot see an animal in its own woodland area unless you have eyes like an eagle's, sharp, sensitive, and searching.

The American Indians were superb woodsmen, but even they knew problems in sighting their quarry. I have no doubt that the white frontiersmen who opened the land for the settlers were the same, because to this day we have knowledge of certain wild plants that the hunters believed would help them to see better, hear better, and better sense the presence of the deer or buffalo or whatever they were stalking.

## *Apocynum androsaemifolium*, spreading rosy dogbane.

When the Menomini Indians were still a primitive society in pioneer Wisconsin days, they believed that the spreading rosy dogbane was a fine hunting magic. They broke a piece from the stalk and sucked it. The magic thereby gained was supposed to coax a deer or buffalo, or maybe even a wild turkey, to the hunter's view and his weapon.

Their neighbors, the Ojibwa, believed that evil spirits were often around the camp and that such evil spirits were a real threat. In such a predicament the Ojibwa looked for the spreading rosy dogbane, dug the plant from the ground, brushed the dirt from the roots, and vigorously chewed a piece of the root. The evil spirits were thwarted. They could no longer threaten an Indian thus protected.

Actually, the stalk and roots and leaves of the spreading rosy dogbane should not be sucked, chewed, or put into the mouth in any

*Apocynum androsaemifolium*, spreading rosy dogbane.

manner. Eating from fifteen to thirty grams of its green leaves has been known to kill a horse or cow. Although the dried rhizome and roots have been taken as an emetic and as a medicine to prevent paroxysms or intermittent fevers by whites and Indians alike, you are warned that such use should be tried only with extreme caution if at all, because the results are uncertain and irregular, even dangerous. It is better to enjoy the plant's beauty and leave its medicinal uses to folklore.

It is a low shrub carrying tiny rosy bells on an extraordinarily clean stem, smooth dark green leaves forming a background. If you pick it, it exudes a white, milky substance that stains your fingers, but it is a beautiful plant when its pink blossoms are nodding in the mid-summer wind.

This dainty shrub belongs to the cooler climate of the northern states or the highlands, where the sun does not bake too hot. It likes open woods and thickets, nodding its pink bells with a delicate rhythm in the breeze.

Dogbane is also known as Indian hemp wherever it might be found, and though the spreading rosy dogbane is a fibrous plant that furnished a fine thread in its outer bark, its value to the Indians lay more in its other qualities than in its fibers.

*Foeniculum vulgare*, fennel.

*Foeniculum vulgare*, fennel.

*Foeniculum vulgare*, fennel.

Juice from the crushed leaves of the fennel was believed to be an eye medicine so good that it would even strengthen the vision. If there is any truth to this old belief, fennel juice in the eyes today should make it easier to spot the movement of big game in the woods.

The use of fennel dates back to the Iron Age. Archaeologists have found fennel seeds mixed with the artifacts of that era. Certainly its history is fascinating and varied. Greek legend links the fennel with Prometheus and Mount Olympus. Roman gladiators were crowned with a fennel wreath and ate fennel before a fight to give them strength.

The fennel may have originated in Europe, but it is found all over America today, a stout, smooth herb growing four to six feet high. The leaves are numerous, with slender thread-shaped divisions. A large umbel with tiny yellow blossoms spread widely apart forms at the tops of stems. The blossoms mature to seeds a quarter of an inch to half an inch long. The odor of both the foliage and the fruit or seeds suggest the smell of anise or licorice.

Popular names include sweet fennel, common fennel, Florence fennel, anise fennel, sweet anise, and ladies' chewing tobacco.

Fennel leaves can be eaten raw, cooked as a green leafy vegetable, or added to soup. They should be used fresh, not dried as the seeds are.

If you do not want to cook the fennel as a vegetable by itself, use a few of the leaves as a flavoring. Bread cooked on a bed of fennel leaves was believed to gather the fennel flavor; the leaves were discarded when the bread was done.

Ancient man used fennel leaves to treat various maladies. Pliny found them handy for treating scorpion stings and mad dog bites, to increase the appetite and sweeten the breath, to help in reducing one's weight, and as an aphrodisiac. Fennel juice from the leaves was dropped into the ears as well as the eyes.

The stalks, like the leaves, can be eaten raw, and were so eaten by children on the West Coast for the pleasant taste. The stalks can be eaten fresh from the plant, added raw to a relish, or blanched in hot water and cooked as a vegetable.

Fennel seeds can be ground into a sort of flour. Drop them whole in cookies or sprinkle them over the tops of plain cookies. The seeds add a subtle flavor to pastries, salads, cold sauces, fish, and candy, and to some liqueurs. Ancient recipes called for fennel seeds to be placed under the crusts of loaves of bread.

Fennel seeds are important in the field of medicine, too. Even in the twentieth century fennel seeds are known as a flavor in medicines and are valued as an additive to modify the action of purgatives. A volatile oil from the seeds is used as a stimulant as well as to relieve gas in the stomach or intestines.

The seeds should be quite ripe and dried before use. Cut them before they scatter and hang them in bunches for further drying. Rub or shake the heads to separate the seeds and store in jars until you need them.

## *Hieracium canadense*, Canada hawkweed.

The Canada hawkweed was considered a valuable hunting charm by the Ojibwa Indians. First they nibbled the root to get the magic within their own bodies and make themselves more alert for hunting; then they used the flowers for a hunting lure. With the roots pulled, the flowers were finished anyway. The complete recipe for the lure has not survived, so it is not certain whether they threw the flowers on a campfire or rubbed them on their traps.

There are some twenty-seven species of hawkweed recognized, but only the Canada hawkweed was assigned such a virtue, possibly because the Ojibwa lived in the northern states from the Niagara River westward to the North Dakota area, and from Wisconsin and Michigan northward about halfway to Hudson Bay. The Canada hawkweed would have been growing in their territory. The word *Ojibwa* was the

*Hieracium canadense*, Canada hawkweed.

*Lactuca spicata*, blue lettuce.

original name of the Indians that was later adapted by the white men to *Chippewa*.

The Canada hawkweed is a small plant, sometimes called the high dandelion because its yellow blossom does resemble an ordinary dandelion blossom, although their leaves are not similar. The leaves are long and lanceolate, with a tendency to clasp the stem, considerably different from the familiar dandelion leaves.

## *Lactuca spicata*, blue lettuce.

I had no problem in finding the blue lettuce to photograph. It was a weed trying to establish itself in my flower garden, and it managed to grow two feet high before I noticed it. We called it milkweed because any broken piece would immediately ooze white fluid that looked like milk but had a wonderful tendency to stain fingers and clothing. If you get that juice on your fingers and inadvertently lick them, you will know the bitter taste of the stuff. I have found no warning of poison in the plant, but that bitterness is going to keep you from chewing very much of it.

In spite of that bitterness, the roots and flowers were both chewed for a hunting charm that was considered to be of some power. If you can stand to chew them, you must be a person of great willpower in the first place, and that faculty will help you get your game anyway.

The blue lettuce grows four or more feet tall; hence its name sometimes is the tall blue lettuce. It has a sedative quality that was valued by some Indians as a medicine to make milk flow easier in a woman's caked breasts after childbirth. They steeped the plant and administered the liquid as a medicine to be drunk by the young mother. White settlers soon learned its soporific quality and occasionally used it for its soothing or calming effect.

The leaves of the *Lactuca spicata* are rather large but deeply cut. The flowers are quite small and not eye-catching. It is not a plant that you would want in your garden.

## *Plantago major*, rippleseed plantain.

## *Plantago rugeli*, blackseed plantain.

A general description of the rippleseed plantain is in the preceding chapter. Both the rippleseed plantain and the blackseed plantain were used advantageously by the hunter.

If you have an earache, press the juice from the leaves and drop that juice in the ear. It will not only cure the pain, but you will also find that your hearing will become sharper the longer you use it. Certainly the sharper your hearing, the better you will be aware of the dainty steps of a deer as it approaches you.

If your tooth, not your ear, aches, chew the roots—the better to eat the venison once you've shot it.

These two plantains have so much in common that they were used interchangeably in the midwestern states. The blackseed plantain is very similar to the rippleseed plantain except for two small items: The shape and color of the seeds differ, and the blackseed plantain has an oblong pod that splits circularly around the base while the pod of the rippleseed plantain is more oval than oblong and splits circularly around the middle.

## *Polygonum muhlenbergi*, bigroot ladysthumb.

The Ojibwa boiled the leaves and stems from the bigroot ladysthumb, which they used not only for stomach pains and as an astringent, but as a tea, potent as a hunting medicine. You will find this a bitter brew, but its known values as a healing medicine for some types of illness may have given the hunter a sense of calm that helped him see the deer or elk he was stalking.

Nevertheless, in Europe there have been cases reported in which horses or cattle have died from eating the raw leaves.

In addition to drinking the tea, hunters tossed the petals of the small flowers into the campfire to make a smoke scent to lure the deer.

*Polygonum muhlenbergi*, bigroot ladysthumb. (Photo from *Weeds of California*, by W.W. Robbins, Margaret K. Bellue, and Walter S. Ball. Courtesy of California Department of Agriculture.)

The root was steeped by the Meskwaki Indians to treat sores in the mouth. Sioux Indians on the plains gathered the roots of several kinds of smartweeds, including this one, and ate them raw or roasted. They taste something like nuts, they say. This report of eating the root is somewhat controversial, as I find another reference in which we are cautioned that the roots of the smartweeds should be avoided, although Muenscher's *Poisonous Plants of the United States* has no warning on the roots.

The leaves in cold water made a tea given to children for the flux, which was the name given to any unusual discharge of fluid from the body.

The *Polygonums* are known as smartweeds because the raw juice of the plants will cause irritation and smarting if it gets in the eyes or nostrils, so bear that in mind.

They are herbs that grow two to three feet high and prefer very wet places for growth. The stems have swollen joints; the leaves are narrow, widest at the base in the *P. muhlenbergi* and tapering to a point. They alternate on the stem, with stipules forming a sheath above the joints. The flowers are on dense spikes from one to four inches long, small blossoms about a quarter of an inch wide.

The bigroot ladysthumb is also called knotweed, swamp persicaria, swamp smartweed, and scarlet smartweed, though the blossoms are pink and not scarlet. It has also acquired the names of kelp, marsh smartweed, devil's shoestring, and tanweed.

## *Prunella vulgaris*, common selfheal.

Make a root tea from selfheal or heal-all, *Prunella vulgaris*, and drink the tea to sharpen your eyes so that you can see the deer slipping through the woods more quickly. The Ojibwa swore this would help, and who knows? It might.

The selfheal is a low-growing perennial with half-inch-long lilac blossoms, sometimes described as being in shades of blue or purple. The short cylindrical flowers grow in dense terminal spikes. The leaves are not big either, rarely growing over a couple of inches long, somewhat oval and occasionally toothed on the edges. Though the plant is not striking in appearance, it had other assets that were known in the primitive days of America.

The plant tops and leaves were administered for fevers. The root, when steeped with certain other plants, was a remedy for so-called "female illnesses." White explorers knew it as a tonic and a medicine to prevent the spasms of cramps or fits. They also believed that it was good for ridding the body of worms, and as a diuretic and a help for the liver. Sore throats and almost any other minor ailment might have been treated by selfheal tea.

The selfheal had various other names, including dragon's head, dragonhead, thimbleflower, all-heal, brownwort, carpenter's herb, carpenter's weed, hook heal, hookweed, heart of the earth, sicklewort, and bluecurls. Some of these common names are also given to several other plants, which is confusing. The only real identification of any of the wild plants is its Latin name.

## *Pyrola americana*, American pyrola.

If you drink a tea made from the leaf of the American pyrola, *Pyrola americana*, it should bring you good hunting luck, too.

You need sharp eyes to find this forest plant, but once you find it you will wonder why you never noticed it before. The blossoms rise from six to twelve inches high on a bare, straight stem, and the waxy white flowers are fragrant as well as quite lovely to see. The basal leaves are somewhat leathery in texture and are more or less rounded.

Because it belongs to the forest where much hunting is done, and because you must have sharp eyes to find this little beauty, it seems appropriate that it belongs to the folklore of the magic associated with hunting for larger game.

It has several other names, including shin leaf, round-leaved American wintergreen, false-leaved wintergreen, larger-leaved wintergreen, pear-leaved wintergreen, Indian lettuce, canker lettuce, wild lettuce, liverwort lettuce, copperleaf, dollarleaf, consumption weed, and round-leaved wintergreen.

*Prunella vulgaris*, common selfheal. (Drawing by Juan C. Barberis from *Plant Medicine and Folklore*, by Mildred Fielder, copyright 1975. Used by permission of Winchester Press.)

*Pyrola americana*, American pyrola.

As you will note, most of the common names are influenced by those round basal leaves rather than by the white blossoms. Two of the names, consumption weed and canker lettuce, lead one to believe that somewhere along the line the American pyrola was used as a medicine to combat consumption and canker as well.

## *Ranunculus pennsylvanicus*, Pennsylvania buttercup.

The seeds of Pennsylvania buttercup were wanted by the hunters, though we do not know how they were prepared or distributed for hunting. It was known as a hunting medicine, which might indicate that the hunter took it internally. Did he eat the seeds, or possibly brew a tea from them?

The entire plant was known to produce a good red dye for fibers or clothing, but they needed bur oak, *Quercus macrocarpa*, to set the color.

*Ranunculus* sp., buttercup. (Photo by Dirk R. Walters.)

*R. pennsylvanicus*, sometimes called bristly crowfoot or bristly buttercup, is a plant from two to three feet high with small yellow blossoms. It prefers moist places, muddy if possible. Its name refers to the bristly hairs on the stems. The leaves are sharply cut and toothed and are divided in three parts.

It is not one of the most flamboyant flowers of the woods or marshes, but its yellow blossoms are a pleasant color against the surrounding greens, and it was lucky for hunting magic.

# 3.

# THE OLD WOODSMAN'S LIQUOR FORMULA

About fifty years ago a dealer in herbs advertised a mixture of wild plants and alcohol that he called Old Woodsman's Liquor. A finely ground mixture of dried berries, roots, and barks, which would blend with alcohol, was packaged with instructions to let one gallon of alcohol and the herbs stand for ten days. The enterprising dealer recommended the resulting brew highly "as an ideal tonic for woodsmen, trappers, hunters and the aged in general."[1]

Well — yes.

He named the herbs in his mixture as rheumatism root, juniper berries, bull nettle root, black cohosh, gentian, Rocky Mountain grape root, and Jamaica ginger, with no further identification. Of course one can hardly blame him for not giving his secret recipe away, but that bunch of names is one of the doggonedest collection of common plant names that I've ever seen.

There were several wild plants believed to aid in curing rheumatism, and at least two were known by the familiar name of rheumatism root: the Atlantic yam, *Dioscorea villosa*, and American twinleaf, *Jeffersonia diphylla*. As far as I can ascertain, either one of these would be safe to take internally.

Fifty-seven species of wild juniper are recognized, plus all kinds of horticultural clones available on the market. We can only assume that any of the blue-berried junipers might be satisfactory.

The only plant I know with the common name of bull nettle is not a nettle at all, but *Solanum carolinense*, officially known as Carolina horsenettle. That must be the one.

Black cohosh can be pinned down fairly accurately. Only one plant

1. Meyer, Joseph E., *The Herbalist*, p. 338.

is called by that name, the *Cimicifuga racemosa*, which is officially the cohosh bugbane, though it has other common names besides black cohosh. There is also a blue cohosh, *Caulophyllum thalictroides*, which is no relation to the black at all, such being the vagaries of the naming of wild plants.

As for the gentian, there are eighty-five known species, so we can take our choice as to which one to add to the brew.

The term Rocky Mountain grape root really throws a curve. Never having heard of a plant with the common name of grape root, first I must assume that he means the root of the Rocky Mountain grape. There is no wild grape tied so closely to the Rocky Mountains that it retains that name. I wondered if the shrub known as Oregon grape might also have the common name of Rocky Mountain grape, so I checked my files and there it was. The Rocky Mountain grape is just another name for *Mahonia aquifolium*, generally known as Oregon grape.

Jamaica ginger is easy; herbalists admit that to be the *Zingiber officinale*. At last we have a definite plant with no question attached. Yet the *Zingiber officinale* does not grow on the American continent unless you happen to find it in the southernmost, tropical areas. I wondered if one of the wild gingers of the American temperate climates, the *Asarum* spp., might have been used as a substitute in the hunter's liquor formula, and it is quite possible that this could be done though the two types of ginger are not related in any way other than their ginger scent and taste. The *Asarum* spp. and the *Zingiber officinale* can be used in the same ways.

We know enough. I'll give you these plants alphabetically, and you can mix them to see what happens. The brew you end up with ought to be powerful enough to give you a relaxing moment after a hard day's hunting.

## *Asarum canadense*, Canada wild ginger.

## *Asarum caudatum*, British Columbia wild ginger.

The Old Woodsman's Liquor Formula calls for Jamaica ginger, and that is *Zingiber officinale*, no matter how you turn it around. Jamaica ginger is a plant grown only in tropical areas of the world, and the United States imports most of its commercial ginger from Jamaica, hence the name. The Old Woodsman found none of it growing in his local woods, you can be sure of that, but I will review the *Zingiber officinale* at the end of this chapter, in its alphabetical place.

In the meantime, botanical references state very plainly that the wild ginger growing in the midwestern states and into Canada was so much like the Jamaica ginger in its scent and spicy root that it was a

*Asarum canadense*, Canada wild ginger (leaves). (Photo by Dirk R. Walters.)

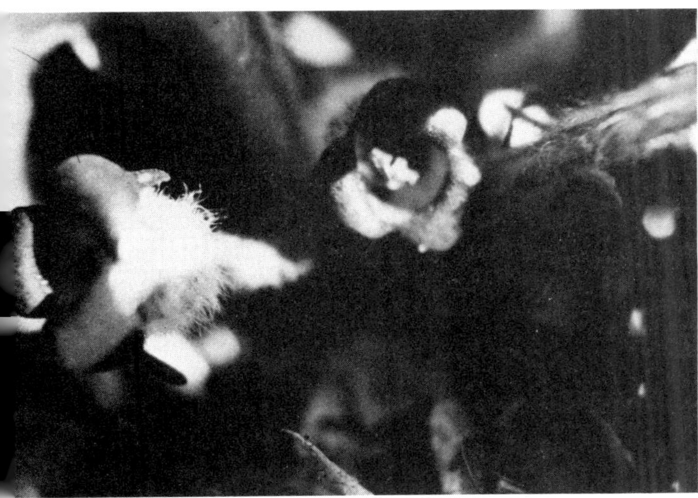

*Asarum canadense*, Canada wild ginger (blossoms). (Photo by Dirk R. Walters.)

*Asarum caudatum*, British Columbia wild ginger.

good substitute for the settlers' wives moving westward with the frontier. The Jamaica ginger and the wild ginger roots were treated alike: candied, ground into spice, cooked green in some recipes, and used as medicines. It is quite possible that you can also substitute the wild ginger roots, properly prepared, in that alcohol tonic.

The wild gingers don't even look like Jamaica ginger, being a group of herbs with creeping stems and spicy-scented leaves that are heart-shaped, two to each plant. The stalks are softly hairy, grayish green, and velvety, and the twin leaves are three to seven inches broad. The flowers grow so close to the ground that they must be searched for and still are hard to find. Purplish brown on the outer side, the flower's inner cup is often creamy white.

Though some of the wild gingers have petals, the Canada wild ginger, *Asarum canadense*, has three long, pointed sepals and no petals, the odd flower growing solitary in the forks between leaf stalks in the early spring.

The root was slightly roasted by Sioux Indians of the Great Plains and put among their clothing so that its fragrance would perfume them.

Midwestern Indians ate the root fresh or dried to treat milk pains in the stomach, or a sore throat or earache if the root was cooked first. They added the root to other foods to make them more palatable. If meat seemed a little spoiled they threw a piece of Canada wild ginger root in the stew to make it taste better. The root was also considered to be a good addition to other plants in making various remedies.

The Canada wild ginger has many common names, depending on the locality. Call it asarum, Indian ginger, Canada snakeroot, Vermont snakeroot, heart snakeroot, southern snakeroot, black snakeroot, coltsfoot snakeroot, false coltsfoot, black snakeweed, broad-leaved asarabacca, wild ginger, or colicroot.

The British Columbia wild ginger, *Asarum caudatum*, is much like the Canada wild ginger in appearance: twin leaves, creeping rootstocks, the strange little blossom hiding in the lower leaves. The flowers are without a corolla, but the calyx has three triangular-shaped lobes, with tips extending in narrow tails one or two inches long. This is a western wild ginger, and you will find it in California and northern states.

Several wild gingers, including both Canada and British Columbia, were made into a medicine by steeping the roots. This was believed to cure whooping cough as well as gas pains in the stomach. The name colicroot obviously came from the latter use. The remedy was made by drying the root, grinding it to a powder much like commercial ground ginger, and adding one-half teaspoon of the powdered ginger root to a cup of boiling water. Take two tablespoons at a time, as often as necessary to soothe the gas pains.

*Cimicifuga racemosa*, cohosh bugbane or black cohosh.

The nine species of *Cimicifuga* are all called bugbanes, but this one is also known as fairy candles, black snakeroot, richweed, rattle weed, rattlesnake root, rattle top, and rattleroot.

It grows a leafy stalk from four to eight feet high, making it highly visible in the woods, especially when the small white flowers are blooming at the top in long, slender racemes from six inches to three feet long. The petals are tiny, only half an inch wide, but there are so many that the fairy candles are easily seen at a distance. They might be striking in appearance, but they also smell bad.

The leaves are large, compound, and sharp-toothed. The plant prefers wooded slopes, and you will find it growing in the East as far north as Ontario and as far south as the Appalachians.

*Cimicifuga racemosa*, cohosh bugbane or black cohosh. (Photo from *Wild Flower Guide*, by Edgar T. Wherry, copyright 1948 by Doubleday & Company, Inc. Used by permission of Doubleday & Company, Inc.)

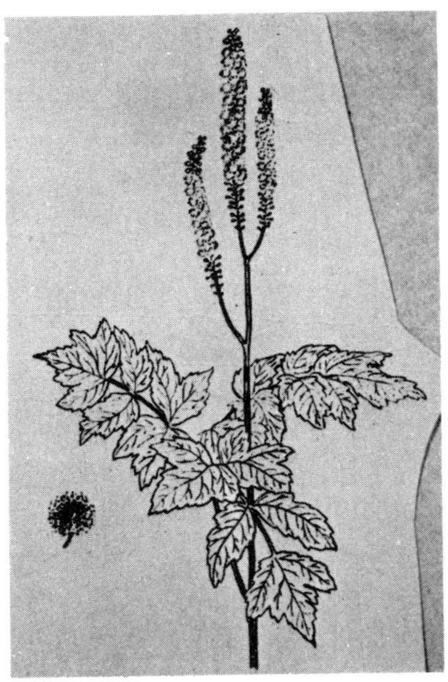

*Dioscorea villosa*, Atlantic yam or rheumatism root. (Photo from *American Medicinal Plants of Commercial Importance*, by A. F. Sievers. U.S. Department of Agriculture.)

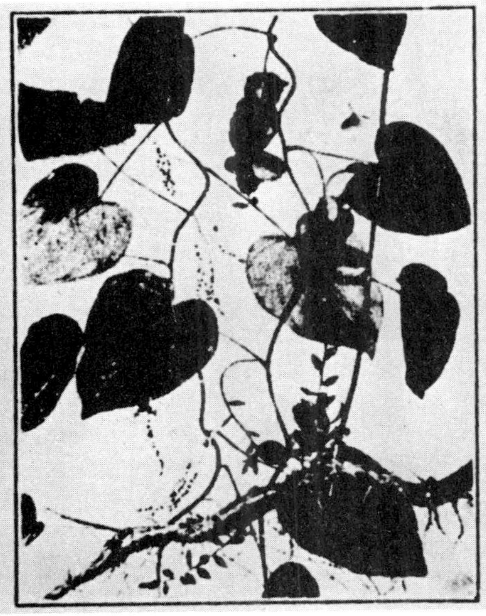

The thick rootstalk has been dried to make a sedative and a tonic, which might be one of the reasons it was included in the Old Woodsman's cocktail. American Indians treated snakebite with the ground roots, which is why it bears the name black snakeroot or rattlesnake root, but white settlers preferred to dry and powder the root to make that bitter tonic.

## *Dioscorea villosa*, Atlantic yam or rheumatism root.

This trailing vine is one of the possibilities for the Old Woodsman's "rheumatism root," though it is also known as wild yam, dioscorea, colicroot, or devil's bones.

The rootstock was the part sought for medicine in early days, as recently as fifty years ago, and possibly even now. It runs horizontally underneath the surface of the ground like a long string, only a quarter to half an inch in diameter. The vine on the surface of the ground trails over adjacent shrubs or bushes, reaching to fifteen feet. The smooth stem bears heart-shaped leaves from two to six inches long and one to four inches wide, hairy on the undersides.

Two kinds of flowers are on the plant. The male flowers droop in clusters, and the female flowers have drooping spikes. Though it bears a fruit, a yellowish green, three-lobed capsule, nothing on the plant is any good to man except that wandering rootstock.

Meskwaki Indians in the Midwest made a root brew to relieve pain at childbirth. White settlers in the area recognized the wild yam root, when simmered, for its medicinal value as an expectorant and to increase perspiration. The root decoction was also administered for bilious colic.

It would appear that the wild yam, with its inherent pain-soothing chemical, had every reason for being in that Old Woodsman's mixture.

## *Gentiana quinquefolia*, fiveleaf gentian.

Of the eighty-five recognized species of gentian, this one is as good as any to toss in that hunter's tonic. White frontiersmen made a beverage from the root for promoting appetite and aiding the digestion, which sounds like a good enough reason to add it to the herbal mixture for the Old Woodsman's Liquor Formula.

The Meskwaki had a more practical use for the root brew. They took a swig of it to stop a hemorrhage, which probably made the sufferer feel more like eating a full meal again as well.

This gentian is also known as stiff gentian, five-flowered gentian, gall of the earth, and gallweed. The last two names may indicate that

*Gentiana quinquefolia*, fiveleaf gentian. (Photo from *Wild Flower Guide*, by Edgar T. Wherry, copyright 1948 by Doubleday & Company, Inc. Used by permission of Doubleday & Company, Inc.)

*Jefferson diphylla*, American twinleaf or rheumatism root. (Photo by Drik R. Walters.)

the plant is not particularly entrancing from the flavor standpoint, but it might have added a zing to the concoction.

*G. quinquefolia* grows from six inches to a couple of feet high, thickly branched along its stalk. The violet-blue flowers are in terminal and axillary clusters, with five petals, each three quarters of an inch long. The blossoms unite in a funnel showing free triangular blades. The leaves are broad at the base but lengthen to a sharp point.

Find it in grassy thickets on thinly wooded slopes in the northeastern, central, and southern states.

### *Jeffersonia diphylla*, American twinleaf or rheumatism root.

The American twinleaf is the other wild plant known familiarly as rheumatism root, that name coming from the medical property of the twinleaf root to relieve rheumatism. Other common names for the American twinleaf or simply twinleaf are Jeffersonia, helmet pod, ground squirrel pea, and yellowroot.

Though the thick, knotty, yellowish brown rootstock growing horizontally under the surface of the ground may still be gathered for medicinal use, I find no other stated illness that the twinleaf is supposed to treat.

The formation of the plant's leaves is interesting. All leaves grow from the base of the plant, sending up long stems about a foot high on which smooth leaves grow, with each leaf blade divided into two wings.

Early in the spring a white flower about an inch in diameter rises about eight inches high from the ground base, bearing eight petals and lasting only one day. As the flower dies, the flower stem keeps growing to eighteen inches high; a pear-shaped capsule then develops to contain many seeds.

If you consider its description, you can readily see why the various common names have developed: twinleaf for the cleft leaf, helmet pod because of the shape of the opened seed pod. Ground squirrel pea would suggest that ground squirrels eat the seeds, and yellowroot is descriptive of the root's color. It was also called Jeffersonia, after Thomas Jefferson.

The name rheumatism root remains, and that alone is sufficient evidence to conjecture that it might be the rheumatism root mentioned by the Old Woodsman.

## *Juniperus scopulorum*, Rocky Mountain juniper.

All junipers have approximately the same values, so it doesn't seem to matter which juniper you find for the Old Woodsman's recipe as long as it has the blue berries instead of the small, hard cones borne by some species. Dry the berries, grind them to a powder, and mix them with the other ingredients. It does not seem reasonable to me to put a potential diuretic in that alcoholic drink, but limiting it to only the berries may have added a tang to the taste without including any possible disadvantage.

The junipers are found from Alaska to Labrador in the north and as far south as Mexico, usually in high hill or mountainous country. On the other hand, I have found the *Juniperus scopulorum*, Rocky Mountain juniper, growing in the arid Badlands of South Dakota, an area as distinctly nonmountainous as you would care to find.

All junipers have short green needles either in overlapping scales on the twigs or, in some cases, pointed like miniature awls. The Rocky Mountain juniper has both types of needles, and it also has the blue waxy berries that are so typical of some of the junipers, though other junipers have strange little bluish or reddish brown cones. The blue berries are edible, though there is little flesh over the seed.

You can eat the juniper berries raw from the bush, or you can

*Juniperus scopulorum*, Rocky Mountain juniper.

simmer a diuretic from the berries and a tea from the scaly leaves or needles.

The Rocky Mountain juniper is found from the Puget Sound in Washington to Arizona; its height depends on the climate and growing conditions. It can stand extreme cold or extreme heat.

## *Mahonia aquifolium*, Oregon grape or Rocky Mountain grape.

Generally known as the Oregon grape, this shrub is also called the Oregon hollygrape, hollyleaved barberry, or California barberry.

Hunters had recourse to the root of this shrub, which grows from two to five feet tall. Oregon grape roots and bark have been used in medicines. The sweet blue berries are edible raw and are good in pies, jellies, and grape juice or grape wine.

Its evergreen leaves are evergreen in the sense that they live from year to year, but in the fall and winter months they turn all shades of red to gleam against the winter snows. During other seasons of the year the leaves are shiny and green and resemble holly in their spiny-toothed edges.

The springtime flowers are bright yellow in drooping clusters. When the flowers are gone those hazy blue berries appear.

The root has been listed in pharmaceutical handbooks as a tonic, and as a medicine to stimulate the liver, prevent periodic returns of

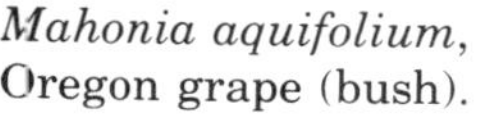

*Mahonia aquifolium*, Oregon grape (bush).

*Mahonia aquifolium*, Oregon grape (leaves and berries).

intermittent fevers or other ailments such as paroxysms, and reduce fevers.

That's quite a potent ingredient to add to an alcoholic beverage.

## *Solanum carolinense*, Carolina horsenettle.

This is the only plant I have found with the common name of bull nettle, though it is also known as sand briar, radical-weed, tread-softly, apple of Sodom, and wild tomato. It isn't even a real nettle. It does not belong to the nettle family but is one of the nightshade family. It has obviously gained the name horsenettle or bull nettle because of the straight yellow prickles that cover the plant.

Berries and leaves of many of the *Solanum* species are reputed to be poisonous if eaten, but one *Solanum* is the common potato, and that we dig for the roots. The root of the Carolina horsenettle is not like the potato, instead being a thick tapering root much branched from the main root stem. I don't know what value it could have possibly added to the Old Woodsman's formula, but there it is.

The Carolina horsenettle is a wild weed that may have had its origins in the Carolinas, but it has spread over much of America by

*Solanum carolinense*, Carolina horsenettle. (Photo by Dirk R. Walters.)

this time, and you will find it even in California, as far west as you can go. Besides the yellow prickles on the plant, the stems are rough and downy, and the leaves are roughened by star-shaped hairs that are more easily seen with a magnifying glass. The leaves are ovate, oblong, and unevenly lobed with wavy margins, from two to six inches long.

The flowers grow in clusters along the stem and are shaped something like potato flowers; they are five lobed, three quarters to one and a quarter of an inch in diameter, bluish white to pale violet. The flowers bloom all summer, but in the fall you will recognize the horsenettle easily by the small round berries, orange-yellow and about half an inch in diameter. They are soft and pulpy like a tomato, and have been dried as an epilepsy medicine.

Sheep eat those berries; humans generally do not.

## *Zingiber officinale*, common ginger or Jamaica ginger.

The common ginger is often called Jamaica ginger because markets in the United States import the best ginger from the island of

*Zingiber* sp., ginger (a horticultural variety).

Jamaica. The plant grows in most tropical areas of the world, though it is native to India.

It is highly unlikely that the Old Woodsman could find common ginger growing in the woods to add to his jug of alcohol. One can only assume that the hunter must either carry along a box of ginger from the local grocer's or use the wild ginger of American woodlands.

The Jamaica ginger is a beautiful plant, the flowers developing from conelike, overlapping bracts of one to three blossoms. Long pinnate leaves grow from the main stem to create a bushy plant some three or four feet tall. The plant grows a year, and then the stem withers, which is a signal to dig the root, the only part of the plant worth harvesting.

Those roots are dried, preserved as candied ginger, or ground. The spice is added to myriad recipes for baked goods, puddings, prepared meats, beverages, pickles—wherever you wish to put it.

This is an ancient spice. References to ginger were made by Marco Polo in the thirteenth century, and in the Talmud before that date. Spaniards brought it to America in the sixteenth century, or at least one or more of the 275 species of ginger. Part of its value lay in various medical remedies.

There you have the Old Woodsman's Liquor Formula: rheumatism root, juniper berries, bull nettle root, black cohosh, gentian, Rocky Mountain grape root, Jamaica ginger, and a gallon of whiskey.

Let the mixture stand ten days, then take a swig, or more if you need it.

Now get to hunting.

# SECTION 2

# HUNTING AND TRAPPING

When that great stretch of land between the Allegheny Mountains and the Spanish missions on the West Coast was one sweeping expanse of virgin woods and prairies, vast numbers of wild animals roamed the miles.

Early explorers gave us some idea of what they saw on their journeys west. When H.M. Brackenridge went up the Missouri River in 1808, he wrote in his journal of seeing buffalo: "About the last of July . . . vast numbers of buffaloes were seen at both sides; as this was near the season when the bulls seek the society of the cows, for at other times they are never seen in the herd; the most tremendous bellowing was heard on every side."[1]

His friend John Bradbury wrote of his own travels in 1809 through 1811, and added the cryptic comment that "they had been able to distinguish where the herds were even when beyond the bounds of the visible horizons, by the vapour which arose from their bodies."[2]

J.B. Wyeth's report of his journey to the Oregon region was published in 1833. He reported seeing more buffalo than he had known

1. Brackenridge, H.M., *Journal of a Voyage up the River Missouri, 1808*, p. 147.
2. Bradbury, John, *Travels in the Interior of America, 1809–1811*, p. 124.

existed: "We saw them in frightful droves, as far as the eye could reach, appearing at a distance as if the ground itself was moving like the sea."[3]

Hunting and hunters being what they are, one can safely assume that the explorers didn't merely look at such large herds unless their camp was loaded with a recently shot stray animal, plenty of food was drying on the jerky line, and there was no need to secure more meat.

Buffalo weren't the only animals around by any means, though man after man spoke of the fine quality of buffalo meat as food. Antelope ran on the plains, and Brackenridge mentions the ploy of a hunter lying flat on the ground while he waved a handkerchief above him on the end of a stick, thus coaxing the curious antelope close enough to be shot. Grizzly bears were not uncommon, and a grizzly would attack a man for little reason. Wolves had a habit of following a hunter, waiting until he had made a kill and stripped the carcass of the meat before they closed in to gnaw on the leavings.

Such herds of buffalo, such overwhelming quantities of animals of all kinds, had to diminish to make room for civilization. Buffalo still exist in the United States but are protected in parks and in private herds. There are thousands of them, and the herds are kept within manageable size by systematic shooting. If you are lucky enough to get a permit, you can still shoot one.

Wolves, bears, and coyotes are not as plentiful for hunting as they once were, but deer are numerous across America even today. White-tailed deer have held their own in numbers through the centuries. There is a fluctuation in the populations of both big game and game birds that has nothing to do with the amount of hunting done. Numbers dwindle, and then they come back in full force another year — a phenomenon that is not completely understood even today.

This book goes back to the days when hunting the big game was necessary to put food on the table. Since wild game was not particularly cooperative in this enterprise, hunters relied on superstition and magic to help them. Much of the magic they knew was connected to the wild plants around them. The lore of some of these plants has come to us complete with intricate directions; the lore of others is less accurate and complete. As I discuss these legendary wild plants, you will see that some of our garden plants and herbs of today are used in much the same manner as the wild ones. You can even buy them in the grocery stores if you don't want to bother with the wildlings. That's not as much fun, but easier.

3. Wyeth, J.B., *Oregon: or a Short History of a Long Journey from the Atlantic Ocean to the Region of the Pacific*, p. 51.

# 4.

# SMALL ANIMALS

If you want to read about a fascinating era, go back to the tales of the mountain men who went into unexplored hills and mountains, following streams to their headwaters to catch beaver and muskrats. These were the years of the 1800s through the 1840s when beaver hats were popular among the gentry in America and England. Big fur companies in the eastern states were headed by men like John Jacob Astor who made millions on the mountain fur business.

You can read about the mountain men's rendezvous in many books (Bernard de Voto's *Across the Wide Missouri* is very good), and imagine that you are hauling your winter's catch of beaver and muskrat pelts, and maybe those of a few other species, to meet with other mountain men whom you have not seen during the long winter snows and the spring thaws. You are going to the rendezvous in the high mountain fastnesses. There you will sell your furs to the traders and celebrate by dancing, boozing with your fellow trappers, and sitting around the campfires while tales are told of grizzly bears and fist-sized nuggets of gold in forgotten creeks and geysers in distant lands. The bears and the gold nuggets and the geysers had a way of getting bigger as the liquor slid down the dry throats of the mountain men. Inevitably the brawls and the fights began, but they were a part of the celebration, too.

It was a riotous era, and it bred men who were half wild and half tame. Those mountain men knew these magic trap lures perhaps as well as the Indians who developed them. The trappers had to know them, because their way of life depended on them.

Castoreum, which is obtained from two pouchlike glands in the abdomen of beaver, is used as a scent bait in beaver traps today, but you can still try the old herbal baits on your traps if you prefer.

## *Arachis hypogaea*, peanut.

Just to ease gently into the problem of baiting traps to catch small animals, peanut butter is excellent bait for most small rodents, to trap mice or rats around the camp, for instance. Even squirrels might be interested in peanut butter, which can help you if you are hungry, since squirrels are a good ingredient in camp stew.

Peanuts are a purely commercial crop these days. The peanut came originally from South America and is cultivated now in the southern regions of the United States because of the congenial climate there. *A. hypogaea* is a small herb bearing short-stemmed yellow flowers and small oval leaves. After fertilization the young fruits go underground and ripen there.

If you forgot to put peanut butter in your camp cooler, try any nut available in the area. Shell them and crush them slightly or break a few nuts to release the aroma, then bait your traps with them.

## *Cornus alternifolia*, pagoda dogwood.

The pagoda dogwood is the dogwood with alternate leaves, and so it is often known by the name alternate-leaved dogwood. The name pagoda dogwood comes from its tendency to form horizontal stages or flats of leaves reminding one of the oriental pagodas known throughout the Far East.

*Cornus stolonifera*, red osier dogwood.

The root of the pagoda dogwood was placed in a muskrat trap to insure that only muskrats were attracted, though this was not the only reason the plant was valued by any means.

The bark made a liquid remedy to be used for piles or as an emetic. In the midwestern states, the dried bark was combined with other barks for an Indian tobacco. Twigs provided thatching materials for summer dwellings.

Most of the dogwoods have a rich, red bark that glows in the spring to signal that sap is running. That bark stays red through the summer, but leaves cover the color so that it is not as obvious as it is in the springtime.

The pagoda dogwood does not have that typical red in its trunk and branches, showing instead a shining light yellowish green that reminds one more of the willows, but the dogwood has oblong dots scattered through the yellow. As they grow older, branches become a rich, polished green striped with gray. The flowers are yellowish white in a branched head, and in autumn the berries are bluish black. This is a beautiful shrub, growing from six to eight feet high in some areas; elsewhere it is a small tree, reaching as high as twenty-five feet.

*Cuminum cyminum*, cumin.

Cumin seed is one of the oldest spices known to man, used before the Christian era began, when it was known to the Persians, the Greeks, and the Romans. Though known almost solely as a food spice, cumin has a bonus for the hunter or fisherman.

Rubbed on baits for either fish or wild animals, it has a tendency to attract fish or game and at the same time mask or kill the scent of human hands. This is a good trick to know, as many wild animals will shy away from human scent. Since cumin is a vegetable product, raccoons, foxes, opossums, squirrels, and rabbits, or similar small animals, might well be attracted to cumin seed as well.

Cumin seed can be used as a substitute for pepper if necessary, though it does not quite match pepper's fiery taste. If you grind the oil seeds there is enough oil in them that the mushy product can be spread on bread for a different-tasting sandwich. The whole or ground seed has been popular for seasoning almost anything in the line of cookery. Appetizers, breads, cookies, cheese, eggs, fish, poultry, game, fruit pies, meats, vegetables — all are benefited by it. It has flavored some liquors or liqueurs and been used in medicines.

The cumin plant grows five or six inches high with a crooked stem. The broad leaves are compound and divided into narrow filaments. The flowers are in heavy cymes of white or lavender petals, so big a cluster that they often weigh the weak stems to the ground.

*Desmodium illinoense*, Illinois tickclover.

The tickclovers have tiny hooked hairs on their fruiting pods, and the hooks cling to clothing, fur, or anything soft that might touch them. These are not burs, but the hooked hairs surely cling as firmly as if they were. This tenacious quality gives it its common name.

The root juice of the Illinois tickclover, also called Illinois tick-trefoil, was placed on traps as a scent lure for small animals. It might have been used for several small animals. Folklore does not mention any one in particular.

There are thirty species of tickclovers recognized and probably more that are as yet unrecognized, but only the Illinois tickclover has come to us with a folklore background. It was also a powerful medicine when combined with other plants, but the recipe was carefully guarded and we do not have it.

Though the blossoms of the Canada tickclover are rather pretty with their purplish color, most of the other tickclovers have flowers quieter in color, and some of them turn greenish as they wither, making them even less noticeable.

*Diospyros virginiana*, common persimmon.

In the South the persimmon is known as the possum tree because opossums go for its ripe fruit. When they have eaten their fill they grab one of the tree's limbs and fall asleep hanging by their tails among the crooked branches. Raccoons like persimmons, too, so it is fairly obvious that if you want to catch a possum or a coon, spread a trap with ripe persimmon fruit. You may have good luck.

The persimmon likes hot weather. It is a slender tree, growing from twenty to a hundred feet high depending on the growing conditions, but it averages forty to fifty feet high. It is also called the date plum.

Though it is a member of the ebony family of tropical trees, the persimmon's wood is only streaked with black, not black throughout. Nevertheless, it is harder than oak, and it has been valued for spinning shuttles in the past, and is used in manufacturing wooden golf club heads today.

The trunk of the tree is straight, but the branches shoot out crazily in all directions. I have not found the persimmon mentioned very often in books on wild plants, but it has never (or rarely) been cultivated on a commercial scale and is generally found growing on its own initiative, wild. It likes dry woods or fields and can be found from Connecticut to Iowa and south to Texas and Florida; I know that it also grows in the hot, dry valleys of California.

The leaves are thick and alternate, dark green and shiny on top

*Diospyros virginiana*, common persimmon.

but a paler green underneath. The yellowish green flowers bloom in May or June, progressing to the oval fruit, which grows to one or one and a half inches in diameter, or larger in some of the thirty-one species listed in America. It is sometimes planted as a source of nectar for honey bees, but the folklore of the persimmon goes back centuries for other reasons.

Persimmon seeds were ground as a kind of flour for making bread; they were also ground and roasted to make a coffee substitute in the South.

The unripe fruit contains tannic acid, and so it was employed as a medicine to combat chronic dysentery and uterine hemorrhage.

The fruit must be nipped by autumn frost to complete its ripening. Fully mature, it was eaten raw by Indians and frontiersmen even as we eat it today. Southern settlers made a persimmon bread, persimmon cookies, and even a persimmon beer.

*Malus coronaria*, wild sweet crabapple.

*Malus fusca*, Oregon crabapple.

*Malus ioensis*, prairie crabapple.

These are wild crabapples, and may by chance be found near your hunting grounds. If you see them, you will know that some of the wild

*Malus fusca*, Oregon crabapple.

*Nepeta cataria*, catnip.

animals in the area have become accustomed to the taste of them and like them.

Cut a chunk of wild crabapple, or of any cultivated apple that you might have in your knapsack, and fasten it to your traps. Muskrats, raccoons, and opossums are particularly attracted to such fruit baits.

Wild crabapples were enjoyed in the wilderness by frontiersmen and made into either sauce or jelly as long as white settlers or Indians could find them. The wild crabapples are still growing in scattered localities throughout the Midwest, but the little tree is rapidly giving way to settled cultivation.

The wild sweet crabapple, *Malus coronaria*, is also called the narrow-leaved crabapple, wild crab, or southern wild crab. The prairie crabapple, *Malus ioensis*, gained only the other names of western crabapple and Iowa crab.

Pioneers knew that the bark could be treated to make a yellow dye, and it is quite possible that Indians of the plains used the bark in the same way. Certainly the Sioux along the Missouri River gathered the fruit for food, and anybody who finds wild crabapples even today would do well to pick them to make jelly.

Meskwaki Indians in Wisconsin thought that crabapples could

cure smallpox, though the apples of course did not do so. They also dried the apples for winter food.

Drive through Oregon today, and you will see miles of the Oregon crabapple growing along the highways, planted there for the beauty of their blossoms.

There is a difference of opinion among botanists over whether the wild crabapples should be called *Pyrus* species or *Malus* species. *Standardized Plant Names* tries to settle the argument by calling all apples or crabapples *Malus* species; pears, *Pyrus* species; and the related mountain ash, *Sorbus* species.

## *Nepeta cataria*, catnip.

Bobcats or mountain lions were predators that sometimes were hunted out of necessity to protect a pioneer's livestock. They were part of the cat family, hence the settlers reasoned, they could be caught with catnip bait. A hunter would make a catnip oil from catnip, *Nepeta cataria*, steaming the herb in a distillation process and then baiting his traps with the catnip oil, which was known to be very attractive to the varmints.

Whatever name you call it — catnip, cataria, catmint, catwort, or catrup — even your household feline likes the stuff, and many playthings made for cats have a touch of catnip secreted in them for the animal's delight.

The leaves are triangular, heart-shaped at base and pointed at the tip. They can be from one to three inches long and are always sharply toothed. The flowers are terminal clusters, or a few may be snuggled among the upper leaves. The corolla is about a half inch long, white or a pale purple. The plant is aromatic, covered with gray hairs and growing from one and half to two feet high.

While the catnip has a decided minty smell to its leaves, it is not a real mint. Like the mints, however, it had its medical day. Catnip tea was brewed for stomach disorders and indigestion. It has a mild sedative quality, which caused it to be used as a sleep-inducing tea for children. Combined with wild mint and peppermint, it was given to combat pneumonia before antibiotics displaced this treatment.

White people of the prairies and hills made infusions of the leaves for several reasons. It was thought to promote menstrual discharge; it also was used to prevent the spasms of such maladies as fits or convulsions. Hot catnip tea was prescribed to expel gases from the digestive tract and was particularly good for colic in infants. It calmed a hysterical person. It purified the blood. It was good for fever and for colds.

If an ill person was suffering from chills, he was plunged into lukewarm bath water in which catnip had been steeped.

*Prunus pensylvanica*, pin cherry.

Besides all that, catnip tea was made just as a pleasant beverage, but how they could accept it for that alone when it was alleged to be good for so many illnesses is quite beyond me.

I understand that even today it is grown commercially in New Hampshire and sold to medicine-makers as a mild aromatic drug.

*Prunus pensylvanica*, pin cherry.

Several small animals and most birds are attracted to cherries and to various kinds of berries. Either they eat the berry itself or they like the aroma or juices. Traps can be rubbed with the berry or cherry juices with good results, particularly if you secure a few of the cherries to the trap for good measure.

Only one little cherry grows light, bright red in all of Canada and the northern tier of states, and that is a tiny one, the pin cherry, *Prunus pensylvanica*. The Latin name generously gives its origin to the state of Pennsylvania, but I have picked it in the Black Hills of South Dakota and made jelly from it wherever I found it.

Many of the other *Prunus* species have fruits as big as small plums, but the little pin cherry is only a quarter of an inch wide at best, yet worth picking in spite of that. The flowers and later the cherries grow a few together in clumps, so you can pick three or four at a time and soon have your pail full. So widely scattered is it over the northern lands that it has gathered other familiar names such as the wild red cherry, bird cherry, fire cherry, pigeon cherry, dogwood, and red cherry.

The pin cherry is a small tree, seldom over twenty-five to thirty feet tall, but it must have light to grow and so is found in cleared spaces along fences or in burned-over spaces, which gives it the name fire cherry.

The pin cherry has a longer, narrower leaf than most of the *Prunus* species, a lance head tapering to a point. The leaves are from three to five inches long and have fine, sharp teeth along the edges. The bark is bright and gleaming, reddish brown marked with faint horizontal stripes, which are in fact lenticels admitting air to the inner bark. That outer bark has a tendency to peel in horizontal strips; underneath it is a green inner bark that smells lovely but is said to be quite poisonous to eat. Muenscher in his book on poisonous plants says that only the leaves are poisonous, but why take a chance? Leave the inner bark alone as well.

Centuries ago the Ojibwa Indians along the Canadian border made a cough medicine from the bark, but whether it was made from the outer or inner bark I do not know. The white settlers in the same area made a bark medicine that they took for stomach troubles, or just as a tonic to make them feel better. One would think from this that the bark could not be too dangerous.

There is absolutely no danger in eating the cherries themselves.

## *Spiraea alba*, narrowleaf meadowsweet.

## *Spiraea salicifolia*, willowleaf spirea.

There are some 120 species of spiraea growing around the United States, and if you refer to the many other names of spiraea, you can come up with even more common names than the Latin ones. If you add all the hybrids and cultivated varieties, it is hardly possible to count the members of the spiraea group today.

The *Spiraea salicifolia*, willowleaf spirea, and the *Spiraea alba*, narrowleaf meadowsweet, were trapping baits when spiraea was just a wild thing in the woods. The Ojibwa rubbed the root juice on their traps and sat back to see what they could catch.

Many of the spiraeas, including the willowleaf spirea, have small white flowers in crowded panicles, though the willowleaf spirea blossoms sometimes have a faint rosy tint as well. The willowleaf spirea is also called the common meadowsweet, American meadowsweet, quaker lady, or queen-of-the-meadows. Generally a bush growing two or three feet high, it is often found in gardens or planted along fences.

*Spiraea* sp., spiraea
(a horticultural variety)

The Meskwaki Indians crushed the immature seeds for a poultice to stop bleeding, but other than that the real reason for the spiraea's being is simply its beauty.

## *Taenidia integerrima*, yellow taenidia.

There is a plant called yellow taenidia, *Taenidia integerrima*, which grows in the Rocky Mountains and foothills near Denver, Colorado, and elsewhere as well. It has the other common names of yellow pimpernel and golden alexanders, names which are applied to other plants as well.

The yellow taenidia had magic for hunting, The root of the yellow taenidia was pulverized and steeped. A hunter made his traps of sticks that he dipped in the liquid as he built the traps. To make the magic certain, he dropped a few seeds in his tobacco pipe or threw them on the campfire. The scented smoke rising through the mountain air was bound to lure muskrats, beaver, or other small animals that the hunter wanted to catch.

Menomini Indians made a root tea for illness in the lungs, so the plant must have grown in what is now Wisconsin, too. The root was steeped, then chewed for bronchial infections. It has a fair taste and so sometimes was combined with bitter plants to improve the taste of the medicine.

### SMALLAGE ROOT BAIT

Common names of plants are sometimes delightful in their connotations, other times absolutely confounding. Listen to this old recipe for a bait that can be used either for trapping animals or as fish bait: "Take smellage root, anise seed, foenugreek seed, and coriander seed. Add a teaspoonful of each to a cup of boiling water. Boil three minutes more, then strain the tea. Place a few drops of this on traps or any kind of bait."

What is smellage root? Wild celery, *Apium graveolens*, has had smallage as one of its common names for centuries. Smallage — smellage. Must be a printer's error (the poor printers are blamed for many things; might as well add this to their burdens). As far as I can find, there is no other plant with a name that even comes close to smellage. So wild celery it is.

Anise seed is the *Pimpinella anisum*. That's easy.

Foenugreek is an old-fashioned spelling of fenugreek, and that, according to all sources, is *Trigonella foenum-graecum*. My etymological reference work defines the word fenugreek as coming from the French word *fenugrec* and the Latin *fenum graecum*, which is translated as "Greek hay."

Coriander seed is no problem. That's the well-known spice *Coriandrum sativum*.

We will discuss these ingredients one at a time, starting with the wild celery, also called smallage.

## *Apium graveolens*, wild celery.

The garden celery that you buy in the stores is a horticultural variety of the wild celery, long cultivated to make the stalks bland and enlarged, edible and sweetened. You will find that the wild celery is juicier and tastier than the garden celery, though it is strong scented and probably should be boiled rather than eaten raw.

The wild celery grows four feet tall under good conditions, though often it is much shorter. The leaves are basal and pinnately compounded into toothed leaflets. The white flowers bloom in compound umbels. The smooth green stem is what you want to eat; it is best to discard the leaves as they contain a high concentration of nitrate. The stalks are hollow and coarse, sometimes sticky to feel.

I find no common names beyond smallage, wild celery, and celery.

In identifying the plant, notice first that it has the odor and taste of celery. It likes wet places and blooms from May to July. These characteristics are important to remember, primarily to be sure that you are not confusing the wild celery with poison hemlock, *Conium maculatum*, which also grows in wet places. Poison hemlock has white umbels of blossoms much like the wild celery and grows even taller than four feet. The poison hemlock has a purple dotted stem, and it stinks. Under no circumstances eat the poison hemlock. It can kill you.

*Apium graveolens*, wild celery.

*Coriandrum sativum*, coriander. (Photo from *Weeds of California*, by W.W. Robbins, Margaret K. Bellue, and Walter S. Ball. Courtesy of California Department of Agriculture.)

*Coriandrum sativum*, coriander.

Coriander was introduced to America from the Mediterranean lands, but it escapes from cultivation often enough that you may find it growing wild. Its seed has a sweet taste and delicate aroma, so it may have been added to the Smallage Root Bait for flavor or scent.

Coriander is one of the herbs longest used in cookery, dating back some 7,000 years. The Chinese, Hebrews, Greeks, and Romans all knew the seed and the root, too. The Chinese boiled the root as a vegetable, but through the centuries that good seed found its way into almost all kinds of cooking from soup to desserts, including the liqueurs or other beverages that might be served as after-dinner drinks. Perfumes were better for coriander seeds, and even some medicines added the seed to make a disagreeable flavor more palatable.

The plant grows one to two feet high, flowering with delicate umbels of white or rosy-tinted blossoms that are often quite pink. The

*Pimpinella anisum*, anise.
(Photo courtesy of
U.S. Department of Agriculture.)

lower leaves may be round or oval, cleft and toothed, but the upper leaves are finely dissected, with the leaflets divided into many narrow parts. The stems are slender and smooth. You might recognize the plant from its strong scent.

The taste of the coriander seed has been described as a cross between lemon and clove, or as a cross between lemon peel and sage. The seed pods or fruits are round. To harvest them, cut the pods as soon as they are ripe. Dry the stalks on trays in a warm place. The seeds will drop from the husks when they are dry, and you can easily separate them from the leaves or pods.

## *Pimpinella anisum*, anise.

Anise is another one of the herbs longest known to man. Historical information links it to mankind's food supply as early as 1500 B.C. The leaves, seeds, and dried flower petals are all used in foods and medicines to this day. Anise is widely cultivated in warm countries in Europe, Asia, and South America.

The foliage is lacy and deeply notched on a plant that grows to an average height of two feet. Those leaves can be added to fruit salads or added to any dish in which you might like a faint taste of anise.

The flowers are fragrant umbels of yellowish white flowers. Pick the petals, dry them, and rub them to a powder, and you have an item that flavors some brands of muscatel and vermouth.

The seeds are the best part of the anise — tiny ovals, greenish gray with blunt ends. They have been used as stimulants or to expel gas from the stomach. In foods, they are added to pastries, desserts, meats, and other dishes. Crushed, the seeds make oil of anise, which is an ingredient of liqueurs, perfumes, soaps, and even fish lures.

### *Trigonella foenum-graecum*, fenugreek trigonella.

The herbalist who mixed the Smallage Root Bait probably had to buy the fenugreek seeds from an import shop, as I can find no indication that it grows in North America except as an occasional cultivated garden herb. It is native to southeastern Europe and western Asia and found in India and in Egypt, as well.

If you check the etymology of the Greek words in the name, you will find that *trigonella* comes from the old Greek word for "triangular," *foenum* is "hay," and *graecum* is "Greek," therefore the combination of words means "triangular Greek hay." The plant is known as fenugreek, fenugrec, or Greek hay and is recognized by *Standardized Plant Names* as fenugreek trigonella.

It has strong-scented leaves and mucilaginous seeds. The seeds were part of medicine at one time, and in India they were used to make a condiment something like curry powder. In Europe it is a medicinal plant, though I cannot find why or for what illness. Certainly it is known as a good forage plant for animals. The leaflets are oblong wedges, triangular in shape. The small flowers, which have yellow or white corollas, grow in the axils of the leaves.

The linear pods are pointed and somewhat curved, two to four inches long, with veiny sides. When they are mature, the seeds are brownish yellow and contain an aromatic oil, starch, and a substance like glue. Egyptians add fenugreek seeds to honey or to bread. The entire plant has been cooked as a potherb in some countries.

There you have it: smallage or wild celery for the base of the mixture, coriander for taste, anise for the attraction that its scent holds for either fish or animals, and mashed fenugreek seeds to make the mixture stick together and adhere to the bait.

# 5.

# BIG GAME

You can buy a deer call today if you want to spend the money. Deer calls have been available for years, but if you want to start a good argument just voice your opinion in a hunter's lodge as to whether or not they are any good.

A deer call that is used improperly, perhaps because the directions are not clear, probably will not be much help in the field. A call that may be effective in one region may not be in another. For example, there is a call that imitates a deer's greeting sound. This works nowhere except in the southwestern states, and even there you'd better have the right kind of greeting sound in that call. In other areas if you rattle a couple of antlers together you'll find the bucks creeping warily up to you to see the fight.

Deer are curious, and before the season begins they are attracted to all kinds of sounds. Lumbermen in the Northwest have testified that deer will come to a camp when they first hear a chain saw echoing through the mountains, but who can use a rifle when he has both hands on a chain saw?

Most hunters will agree that you can fool ducks with a duck call. You can fool a turkey with a turkey call. But you had better know what you are doing to make a deer call work.

Years ago, when the wild woods of America were hunted only by Indians or by white frontiersmen, the red men and the white hunters had their own theories on what to do about a deer call.

You simply had to use the right plants, they said.

It may be against the law in some areas to use bait to attract big game, but a couple of plants are known today that will coax a buck to a stand and keep him there while you get your sights on him. If this is illegal where you hunt, then read this chapter only for its historical interest.

*Asclepias syriaca*, common milkweed.

*Eupatorium perfoliatum*, boneset.

*Asclepias syriaca*, common milkweed.

You may have a proper deer call in your pocket. If you do, it will work better if you put milk from the stems of common milkweed, *Asclepias syriaca*, on it. I don't know why, but Indians in north central America said it would work.

The milkweed is a wonderful plant, if everything credited to it is true. First of all, it is one of the most edible plants in the wild woods. From the moment when the first shoots or sprouts appear in the spring (when you can cook those sprouts like asparagus and eat them) until the seeds are in the pod, you can cook that milkweed in all of its parts. You can serve the boiled milkweed like a bowl of greens. You can toss it into a buffalo-meat stew. You can combine it with dried green corn. You can cook the pods, the buds, the leaves, and the tips of the stalks, and all are good — except when the milkweed is growing in soil containing selenium. In that case you might get selenium poisoning because of the amounts the plants have absorbed from the soil.

The milkweeds, with their big umbels of blossoms, are such pretty plants that one does not like to think of any danger in them. The common milkweed blossoms vary between a greenish purple and a greenish white. Its leaves are white and woolly on their undersides.

Fiber has been stripped from the stalks for weaving purposes. A root tea was believed to be good for any pains inside the body. The fluffy seeds were picked by French Canadians and stuffed in bags to make mattresses, which gave it the French name *cotonnier*, meaning "cotton for stuffing."

Other names are silkweed, silky swallowwort, Virginia silk, and wild cotton.

## *Eupatorium perfoliatum*, boneset.

If you do not have a deer call, you can make one that will whistle the deer to your side very effectively. You will need boneset to help. Dig the roots of both boneset and milkweed, *Asclepias syriaca*, but strip the root fibers of the boneset. Combine the milkweed roots with the root fibers from the boneset as you would to make any whistle; the resulting whistle sounds like the call of a deer.

Boneset gains its common name from the appearance of the leaves on the stems. The stems seem to pierce through opposite leaves that join at their bases, giving the appearance of one long leaf extending from one side of the stem to the other, thus suggesting that a plant with such united leaves should heal fractured bones.

Such a powerful plant certainly had its other medicinal uses as well. The plant tops and leaves were brewed and taken in small amounts to lower a fever. If administered in a large quantity, the brew was a bitter laxative. Whites took the boneset tea in small doses as a stimulant, an emetic, and diaphoretic to produce perspiration. It was good for colds, bronchitis, sore throats, and acute inflammations. The leaves made a tea that got rid of worms in the body.

The Meskwaki Indians called it snakeroot because they believed it would cure a snakebite. On the other hand, Indians in New England claimed to cure typhus fever with the boneset.

The plant can grow five feet tall, but the ones I found were about three feet high. The small blossoms are rather soft to the touch, a panicle of white at the top of those united leaves. The blooms make a good nectar for honey, so bees search for boneset flowers with enduring energy.

## *Heracleum lanatum*, cowparsnip.

The entire herb of the cowparsnip was a hunting necessity for the Menomini Indians of early Wisconsin.

If you burn the lower stalk, the resulting ashes are a good salt substitute. Farmers will put a salt block in the cow pasture to give the cattle a salt lick, so it is quite possible that if you spread some of those salty ashes in a convenient spot you will have a salt lick to attract deer or any other big game.

I am not sure whether or not that is legal today. This book does not contain information on hunting regulations, merely on folklore.

The cowparsnip is a big plant growing near streams, hard to ignore when you see its giant leaves and the flattened white tops of its flowers. It reaches eight feet tall, with leaves often a foot or more long and wide. You can spot the cowparsnip from quite a distance because no other streamside plant has the flat white umbels of flowers on top of such enormous leaves.

For some time there has been a controversy among botanists as to whether or not cowparsnip leaves are poisonous to cattle, but the majority opinion today seems to be that they are not. Whether or not the leaves poison cattle, some parts of the cowparsnip have been prescribed as medicines. Along the Missouri River, the big tops have been smudged in a campfire to counteract fainting and convulsions. The Indians there scraped the root, which they pounded and boiled to make a poultice for boils. They also boiled the root for intestinal pains.

Several midwestern tribes thought it was a good medicine. The root was supposed to cure epileptic fits and was given for colic and cramps in the stomach; it also had a reputation as an erysipelas cure and as a poultice for sores. The seeds were taken for a headache. On top of all that, they cooked the root and ate it for food.

Lewis and Clark on their memorable journey up the Missouri River to the West Coast found the Wollawollah Indians eating the inner

*Heracleum lanatum*, cowparsnip.

parts of the stem; so the exploration party ate it too and found it very good. On the far West Coast the young stems, flowers, and roots were all cooked and eaten.

In spite of all these blessings, the Menomini also considered it to be an ingredient in an evil medicine made by their sorcerers.

The cowparsnip has other common names: masterwort, cow cabbage, and hogweed. Most people, though, know it as cowparsnip.

## *Levisticum officinale*, lovage.

Reports circulate that the root of wild parsley will attract animals, big or small, primarily because of the aromatic odor of the root. Finding this valuable item presents a problem, since at least three wild parsleys exist. Such is the confusing state of common names.

One of the wild parsleys is the common garden lovage, *Levisticum officinale*, which is also a definite ingredient in a recipe included in Chapter 12, "Fish Baits." The species of the genus *Lomatium*, which have edible roots, are also called wild parsley or biscuitroot. The third wild parsley is the *Zizia aurea*, golden zizia. The root of the *Zizia aurea* has been part of a fever remedy in primitive areas of America, but I find no reports of its edibility, so we may ignore that one.

Lovage has been cultivated for so many years as a garden herb that it has even acquired the name garden lovage. It came from Europe, where the Benedictine monks in Switzerland grew it for food. Greeks and Romans knew it, and our ancestors brought the lovage to New England. It may escape to the wild state, but it is still more likely to be found in our gardens. Through the centuries it has been called love parsley and wild parsley, as well as lovage. It grows five to seven feet high, a smooth plant, sweet and aromatic to smell.

All parts of the herb were used. The thick dark brown root was candied and eaten or used to flavor tobacco blends and perfumes. The round, hollow stalk and stems can be blanched as celery stems are today, then eaten raw or cooked. The coarse, heavy leaves are large and compounded or divided, wedge-shaped with cut or lobed leaflets. When they are young and tender the leaves can be added to cooked foods or served raw in salads.

For use in the animal bait, the root was likely the part of the lovage to be used because of its aromatic scent. If it could flavor such strong items as tobacco and perfume, it would surely have a scent or flavor strong enough to attract animals.

When the lovage blooms it produces umbels of many small greenish yellow flowers, which mature to brown-headed umbels of seeds. Those seeds are tiny, about the size of caraway seeds but different in shape. Lovage seeds are slightly curved, smooth inside and with a

*Lomatium* sp., biscuitroot. (Photo by Henry W. Meyer.)

single rib on the outer side. The seeds have long been known for their sweet taste as well as for their good scent. Baked goods, candies, meats, and salads can all be improved by a bit of lovage seasoning from whole or ground seeds.

### *Lomatium foeniculaceum*, hairy parsley or fennel lomatium.

### *Lomatium simplex*, narrowleaf lomatium.

All of the lomatiums are part of the parsley family and were also called wild parsley, which puts them in the category of an animal bait of some kind. They were also more generally known as biscuitroots, because of their edible roots, which could have been part of the bait. Though most lomatiums have finely dissected leaves like carrots, the various species differ in many details.

The *Lomatium foeniculaceum* is officially given no common name, but the Latin name *foeniculaceum* means "like the fennel," and some botanists have given it such names as love seed, hairy parsley, wild parsley, biscuitroot, carrot-leaved parsley, or fennel lomatium.

The leaves are hairy and finely dissected, which gives it the name of hairy parsley. The leaves of some species are cooked as greens, and this may have been one of them. The flower umbels at the tops of the stems are yellow, but it seems they have never served any purpose other than beauty. The seeds were part of a love charm used by Missouri River Indians.

The narrowleaf lomatium, *L. simplex*, is sometimes called the nine-leaf species, biscuitroot, or hog fennel. It is valued as a forage plant in the western United States. Its reputation as a forage plant certainly indicates that animals feed on the leaves if not the root.

*L. simplex* also has small umbels of yellow flowers, but the leaves are narrow and slender, like grass.

The root is the most important part of the lomatiums. Thick, rounded, and bulblike, the roots are so edible that the name biscuitroot applies to all species. These roots have been cooked as vegetables, baked, roasted, and eaten raw. Dried, they have been ground into a flour for bread.

### *Malus coronaria*, wild sweet crabapple.

### *Malus fusca*, Oregon crabapple.

### *Malus ioensis*, prairie crabapple.

A general description of the crabapples is found in Chapter 4, "Small Animals."

If you are a deer hunter, you might want to know that deer are particularly attracted to apples, though this attraction is not limited to wild crabapples. Any apple orchard will lure deer. Deer's love for apples is so well known that you can buy a bottle of apple scent from a sporting goods store if you are not sure of finding frostbitten apples on the ground. The apple-scent lure is effective only where apples grow, as deer's taste for frostbitten apples (or fresher apples) is an acquired one.

You may carry apples as part of your day's lunch or as snack food, then toss the cores near your deer stand quite legally. The cores are biodegradable and therefore not ecologically objectionable even if the deer do not eat them.

The strong odor of frostbitten apples turning brown on the ground is even more attractive to the deer than whole apples. If you can find some rotting apples under a tree, grab them. Rub some of them on the soles of your boots, toss a dozen or more around the spot where you hope to see a deer, then sit back and wait.

Experienced hunters say it works.

# 6.

# SMOKE SCENTS

Hunters gathered a few plants that gave off a pervasive scent when mixed together and burned. These plants were either smoked in a pipe or dropped in a campfire to mingle with the coals. Either way, the scented smoke drew deer to the hunting area; this was considered hunting magic.

One of these plants was *Taenidia integerrima*, yellow taenidia, which I mentioned in Chapter 4, "Small Animals," but the smoke of several other plants also attracts animals.

American Indian tribes in many parts of the country did not have modern tobacco to stuff into their pipe bowls. Depending on the area and the purpose, various tribes had their own ideas of what constituted a good smoke.

Many tribes throughout the midwestern and plains areas shared a quarry in Minnesota in which they found red pipestone, an excellent rock for shaping into a bowl for a smoking pipe. Because of their reverence for that particular mineral, the tribes frequenting the spot lived and worked peacefully side by side as long as they were in or near the red pipestone quarry.

The pipes that they carved from the stone were often the peace pipes shared among the leaders of Indian or Indian–white conferences, but the idea of smoking a pipe filled with some distinct wild plant to attract a deer could have been just as important to them as smoking's ceremonial uses were.

Did you ever enter a house and immediately know from the scent in the air that the fireplace logs were of fragrant walnut wood, or perhaps apple wood? The logs produce a cozy incense that tells you immediately that comfort and ease are to be found in that house.

There's something about the smell of the smoke from a fragrant fire.

*Arctostaphylos uva-ursi*, bearberry.

*Arctostaphylos uva-ursi*, bearberry.

The bright red bearberries of snowy woods were burned in an Indian campfire to coax deer and other animals close to a hunter.

The *Arctostaphylos* has the distinguishing Latin addition of *uva-ursi* which translates literally to bear's grape or bearberry. We recognized this trailing ground cover wherever we saw it in the Black Hills of South Dakota, both because of its urn-shaped flowers which belong to the heath family and because of the brilliant red berries which appear in the autumn among the bright green of the leaves. Those red berries cling to the branches for months. We picked them to put among the green of firs and spruces when decorating our homes for Christmas. They were our version of Christmas holly when we had no holly for decoration. Bearberry grows from the Arctic regions extending south as far as northern California or Virginia, particularly liking mountain country.

Bearberry leaves were part of the Missouri River Indian tribes' tobacco in a day when no other tobacco was available. They mixed the dried leaves with sumac, red osier and other dogwoods, and called the product kinnikinnick, so the name kinnikinnick (spelled variously) came to be the name of the bearberry itself.

The tannin in those bearberry leaves also is valuable for curing pelts; even today leaves are gathered in Russia for the tannin. The tannin appears in an extract left by brewing the leaves, making an astringent medicine for catarrh and urinary diseases.

The dried leaves were treated by Wisconsin Indians as a seasoner to make female remedies taste better, but the white settlers found many more medical virtues in the dried leaves. The acid extract has diuretic, tonic and astringent properties, and was prescribed for inflammation in urinary diseases, for chronic bronchitis, diarrhea, leucorrhoea, menstruation problems and uterine hemorrhages.

Bearberry is so well known where it grows that it has acquired many common names. Know it also as uva-ursi, red bearberry, bear's grape, bear's bilberry, bear's whortleberry, foxberry, upland cranberry, mountain cranberry, crowberry, mealberry, rockberry, universe vine, brawlins, burren myrtle, sagachomi, and rapper dandies.

## *Aster cordifolius*, heartleaf aster.

## *Aster macrophyllus*, bigleaf aster.

These two asters were smoked in a pipe to attract deer, the hunter hoping that the smoke would waft gently over thickets where deer might be browsing. Roots of both asters were also burned in a campfire for the same purpose.

The heartleaf aster, *Aster cordifolius*, is smooth and much branched, with rather thin, toothed leaves and many small loosely panicled heads of pale blue or whitish flowers. Its name comes from the heart-shaped leaves toward the lower ends of the stems, but it has another common name arising from the bluish tint of the blossoms: blue wood aster. As far as I have found in research, the heartleaf aster's only claim to fame is that it has been used as a hunting charm.

The bigleaf aster, *Aster macrophyllus*, is also called large-leaved aster. It is larger and stouter than many of the other asters, with broader and rather rough, thick leaves. Its blossoms are white and rather few to a plant. It, too, has a few heart-shaped leaves.

The bigleaf aster had one or two uses other than as a hunting charm. The ancient Ojibwa Indians made a tea from the root with which they bathed their heads when they had headaches. If no one had a headache, they tossed the root into soup for eating. If the leaves were young and tender, they ate them, too.

There are some 136 wild asters recognized by botanists, besides several hundred horticultural varieties.

## *Cicuta maculata*, spotted waterhemlock.

Spotted waterhemlock, *Cicuta maculata*, was considered to be a good hunting lure if the root, not the seeds, was added to the campfire and allowed to smolder. This spotted waterhemlock has its niche in folklore, but I wouldn't touch the thing.

The root and rootstocks are the most poisonous parts of all *Cicuta* species, no matter where you find them, and that is poisonous indeed.

*Aster macrophyllus*,
bigleaf aster.

*Cicuta maculata*,
spotted waterhemlock.

Eating any portion of the plant can kill you, and though inhaling smoke from the burning root has not been proved poisonous, who wants to be the guinea pig in order to find out?

*C. maculata*, a coarse plant growing a couple of feet to several feet high, is usually found near swamps, wet thickets, or little streams. It likes water. The white flowers are in a compound umbel. The leaves are pinnately divided on opposite sides of the stem, each leaflet nearly three inches long and coarsely toothed. Watch for purple spots or streaks on the stems, and take a good sniff. The plant has a most peculiar odor, rather unpleasant.

Spotted waterhemlock is known by several other common names: water hemlock, American poison hemlock, musquash root, musquash poison, spotted hemlock, spotted cowbane, beaver poison, children's bane, wild parsnip, snakeweed, western waterhemlock, and cowbane.

## *Crataegus* spp., hawthorn.

You must burn the bark of the hawthorn, *Crataegus* spp., in that deer smoke, and watch that you do not impale yourself on the sharp thorns while you gather the bark.

There are a tremendous number of hawthorn species around America. Some botanists insist there are up to 1,200 species in the United States; others claim that this is too definitive and that many of the species should be lumped together. However many species there may be, the fruits of all of them are very edible.

These are shrubs or trees growing from five to thirty feet high. The leaves are somewhat roundish overall but have sharp or round shallow lobes and are finely toothed besides. They vary in length from one to three inches. The flowers are white, and most have dark red fruit with two stones or seeds.

The main distinguishing mark of the hawthorns are those wicked thorns from one to five inches long. Primitive Indians in the northeastern United States gathered those thorns and made needles for sewing buckskins from them — that's how sharp and strong they are. They will go through your skin as easily as they did through that buckskin.

The fruit and the bark were once a woman's medicine if steeped into some kind of beverage. The berries alone, besides being quite edible, were believed by white settlers to have certain astringent and medicinal values for heart trouble.

The berries remind one of small apples, hence the name apple has crept into some of the common names by which members of the genus *Crataegus* are known — for instance, red haw apple and thorn apple. The thorns have inspired many names: thorn plum, thorn apple, river hawthorn, thornbush, western black hawthorn, thorn, hagthorn, white thorn, and cockspur thorn. The appropriateness of these names will strike you the first time you attempt to gather the berries. Other names by which hawthorns are known are haw, red haw, mayhaw, and scarlet haws.

### *Erigeron canadensis*, horseweed fleabane.

### *Erigeron philadelphicus*, Philadelphia fleabane.

Two of the fleabanes were smoked in a pipe for a hunting lure, the Philadelphia fleabane, *Erigeron philadelphicus*, and the horseweed fleabane, *Erigeron canadensis*.

The fleabane and the aster are very similar in appearance, both bearing small flat blossoms that grow in loose panicled heads, each blossom about an inch in diameter. However, there is a difference. One of my botanical friends showed me that difference when I was still struggling to learn one flower from another.

"See?" she said, holding an aster in one hand, a fleabane in the other. "The aster has a row of neatly spaced petals around its center, quite easily counted, but the fleabane has so many narrow petals that you cannot count them at a glance."

So there you are, no problem at all telling the two apart.

The fleabane is crowded with those fine petals, and though technically speaking you could count them, the illusion is that they are innumerable.

Of the sixty-five species of fleabane definitely recognized by botanists, *E. canadensis* and *E. philadelphicus* were imbued with hunting magic. If you are in the woods and hunting for meat, large game like deer or elk perhaps, you need the disk florets from either the Philadelphia fleabane or the horseweed fleabane. Tuck the flowers in your pipe and puff the smoke slowly into the air. Maybe it is the scented smoke that gets game, or maybe it's just magic, but old-time hunters believed that one way or another the fleabane smoke was a potent lure.

The horseweed fleabane was a steaming agent in a sweat bath as well as a hunting lure. White pioneers thought the dried leaves and flowering tops made a good astringent and styptic, increased perspiration, and could be steeped in a medical tea for dropsy and bronchitis. It was also used as an expectorant and as an intestinal astringent for diarrhea.

The Philadelphia fleabane was principally a cold or fever medi-

*Erigeron canadensis*, horseweed fleabane. (Photo courtesy of U.S. Department of Agriculture.)

*Erigeron philadelphicus*, Philadelphia fleabane.

cine. The disk florets were gathered by Meskwaki Indians, powdered, then sniffed up the nostril, making the patient sneeze and thereby breaking up a head cold. If that didn't work, they dried the flowers, smoked them, and inhaled the smoke. That smelled so good that they sometimes added the dried flowers to their pipe tobacco just for the pleasure of it. The flowers were also steeped in a tea that was drunk to break the fever sometimes accompanying a cold.

To compare the two fleabanes, the Philadelphia fleabane has stem leaves broad and clasping by a heart-shaped base; its little blossoms are pink.The horseweed fleabane has white blossoms, and the linear leaves are hairy to the point of being bristly.

Though the Philadelphia fleabane seems to have only the one common name, the horseweed fleabane has gathered many names, depending on the area in which it is found. Know it as erigeron, mare's tail, Canada erigeron, butterweed, bitterweed, cow's tail, colt's tail, fireweed, bloodstanch, hogweed, prideweed, or scabious.

Even as late as 1930 the horseweed fleabane was gathered to distill an oil of erigeron for commercial use.

## *Polygonum muhlenbergi*, bigroot ladysthumb.

A general description of the bigroot ladysthumb is in Chapter 2, "Sharpen Your Senses."

The flowers of the bigroot ladysthumb are the thing to smoke for a deer-hunting charm. Throw them into a smoking campfire, and the breeze will take the scent to the deer.

Of course, if you have the plant on hand you might also try the ancient Ojibwa practice of drinking a tea made from the leaves and stems. This should put you in the right mood for bagging your buck.

## *Pseudotsuga taxifolia*, Douglas fir.

The majestic Douglas fir is America's second tallest tree, sometimes reaching over 200 feet high. It has such strength in its wood and such beauty in its straightness as it climbs toward the sky that it is no wonder the tree was known as magic to the hunters and fishermen of bygone eras.

It was believed that if any ordinary bow and arrows, no matter what they were made of, were passed through the smoke made by Douglas fir boughs placed on a campfire and a hunter's chant was sung at the same time, no deer would be able to smell that hunter approach. Being thus able to move close to a feeding buck, a hunter was almost sure to get his deer.

*Pseudotsuga taxifolia*,
Douglas fir.

This great tree is abundant along the coast ranges of the West. It was known by Indians there for many reasons, but even they hewed planks from the trunks to build their homes. Today at least two thirds of the lumber from the Northwest is the Douglas fir, sometimes going under the name of Oregon pine or Douglas spruce.

This is not a true fir. The cones droop from branches; the cones on the true firs are erect. The short needles of the Douglas fir are flat, soft, and blunt, a rich yellowish green.

Some of the other things made of Douglas fir wood included climbing hooks for climbing the tall sugar pines and digging sticks for gardening purposes. Smaller roots were fine for weaving baskets if they were split into numerous strands. The fresh young needles were steeped in hot water to make a hot drink much like coffee, a drink known to both Indians and whites. The tips of the branches were boiled to treat tuberculosis or other lung troubles.

Rheumatism victims underwent a rigid treatment in a sweat house made from Douglas fir branches laid on hot rocks and covered with earth. A blanket over the branches eased the bed for the patient, and after half a day on that sweat box any rheumatism just gave up. If the

*Rumex crispus*, curly dock.

rheumatism was severe, the medicine man waved Douglas fir branches over the suffering victim and chanted charms to make the medicine work better.

Indians gathered Douglas fir gum and burned it in a hollow tree. The accumulating soot made a strong black dye for tattooing the skin.

Western explorers in the early days knew that Douglas fir was a marvelous source of tall, straight trunks for ship masts and spars. It is strong, able to bend with the wind without breaking.

Truly, the Douglas fir can be said to be one of the trees that made the Northwest great.

## *Rumex crispus*, curly dock.

Throw the brown seeds of *Rumex crispus*, curly dock, into the fire to join the smoke of the others. The curly dock seeds grow so thickly that you can gather a handful in a single clutch of your fist.

*Rumex crispus* has been valued for many reasons, one of them being that the leaves are quite edible if they are cooked alone, with split peas, or in stews. You may know the plant as sour dock, dock, curly-leaved dock, sorrel, curled dock, yellow dock, or rumex. When I was a child I was sure it was Indian tobacco because of the appearance of the seeds, and I have learned since that other children thought the same thing.

Actually, the brown seeds were once ground into flour and then cooked in small cakes over a campfire. And the edible green leaves were once used raw as a poultice by the Sioux tribes. The root was valued in the Wisconsin area as an astringent poultice to heal cuts. Even in twentieth-century pharmaceutical handbooks you might find reference to the curly dock roots as an astringent or tonic, or even as a medicine to combat diseases of the lymphatic glands.

Quite a plant, this curly dock. No wonder the Ojibwa figured it ought to be good for hunting magic as well.

## *Sium suave*, hemlock waterparsnip.

Several plants were added to a campfire to make a smudge that was effective. Some, like the hemlock waterparsnip, *Sium suave*, were searched for their seeds only, which were thrown into the fire to drive away the evil spirit that steals a hunter's luck.

Some people know this plant just as hemlock; others use only the name waterparsnip. It has been suspected of being a poisonous plant, but botanists do not confirm this. The *Sium suave* looks much like the very poisonous *Cicuta maculata*, spotted waterhemlock, and grows in similar circumstances near water, which is reason enough to leave it

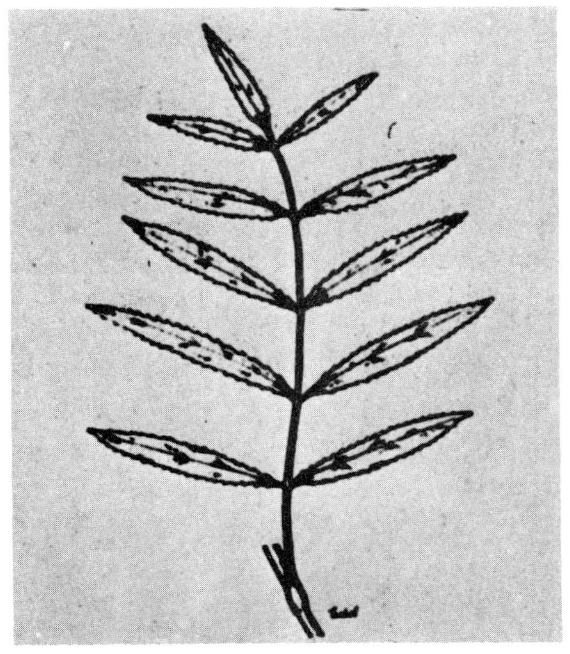

*Sium suave*, hemlock waterparsnip (leaf detail). (Photo from *Weeds of California*, by W.W. Robbins, Margaret K. Bellue, and Walter S. Ball. Courtesy of California Department of Agriculture.)

alone if you question its identity. Both have the same type of deep green daggerlike leaves, narrow and jagged on the edges. Both have white-topped umbels of small blossoms. They can easily be mistaken for each other.

The obvious differences are in the leaves and roots. The leaves of the hemlock waterparsnip grow opposite each other like the parts of a feather, but the leaves on the spotted waterhemlock are spread from the main leaf stem in groups of three or five.

A toxic yellow oil exudes from the broken roots of the *Cicuta* spp., but not from the *Sium* spp.

## *Solidago graminifolia*, grassleaf goldenrod.

Several goldenrods were known to have medicinal value in frontier days, but apparently only the flowers of the grassleaf goldenrod were needed as a hunting lure. The Ojibwa put them in the campfire to smoke the deer from his haunts. Since goldenrod blooms are generally a good indication that summer is ending and autumn is just around the corner, goldenrod smoke would be quite appropriate today, when deer-hunting season is an autumn sport over most of the mountain areas.

The grassleaf goldenrod flowers were also boiled to make medicine for a pain in the chest. It would also expel gas from the alimentary canal, thus relieving such ailments as colic and griping of the stomach. It prevented spasms, and it was an intestinal astringent.

With all this, the grassleaf goldenrod has gathered only a very few other common names. Know it as fragrant goldenrod, bushy goldenrod, and flat-topped goldenrod. There are several other species of goldenrod that also have flat tops, so that last name is not a positive identification for *S. graminifolia.*

The grassleaf goldenrod has narrow, straight leaves like grass, and the flat-topped group of small florets is yellow, as in all the goldenrods. It belongs to the eastern half of America and grows in damp thickets.

## *Tanacetum crispum*, curlyleaf tansy.

## *Tanacetum vulgare*, common tansy.

Gather the tansy flowers, those little yellow buttons that you see along the highways in the fall, and add them to your campfire when you are hunting deer during the autumn hunting season. The scent of the tansy blossoms in the smoke will lure your game to you, just like magic.

Tansy's vivid yellow buttons topping dark fernlike leaves are seen along the highways from midsummer to fall. Grown in herb gardens

*Solidago graminifolia*, grassleaf goldenrod. (Photo from *Wild Flower Guide*, by Edgar T. Wherry, copyright 1948 by Doubleday & Company, Inc. Used by permission of Doubleday & Company, Inc.)

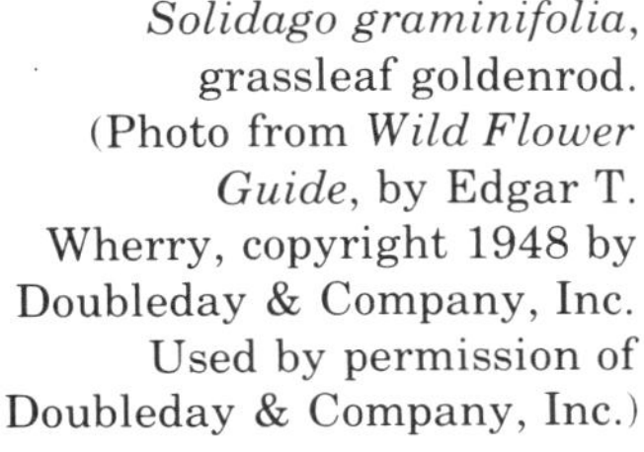

*Tanacetum vulgare*, common tansy.

since the days of Charlemagne, it has escaped to grow wild today across America. I have seen tansy growing solidly in acres, and flanking a woodland highway for a couple of miles or more. Once started, tansy likes to spread and does so with ease.

Common tansy has accumulated a few popular names that may ring a bell for you, including bitter buttons, ginger plant, English cost, parsley fern, scented fern, and hindheal.

It was once made into a cosmetic, a tansy lotion that was supposed to get rid of freckles. Gather the tansy leaves fresh and green and soak them in buttermilk for nine days. Apply the lotion for a week or more. If you can believe the folklore of backwoodsmen, those freckles will fade and fade.

If you have any tansy leaves left, you can put a sprig on every shelf of the kitchen cupboards, and the ants will keep out of those shelves, certain as fate. I guess that isn't really magic. It works because ants do not like tansy leaves.

Tansy was used in tansy cakes, puddings, and tea, and it was served in spring to insure good health. An old recipe suggests that we use tender young leaves sparingly with fish or meat. Tansy tea was once believed to calm the nerves.

Two varieties of tansy are valued, the common tansy, *Tanacetum vulgare*, and fern-leaved tansy or curlyleaf tansy, *Tanacetum crispum*. Five others are listed, but they are not as well known as these two. Both varieties have been used for their medicinal or industrial value; they are part of cosmetics, toilet waters, and ointments, and are even an ingredient in Chartreuse liqueur.

One can dry tansy buttons for winter bouquets, and the golden yellow of the flower heads will stay bright all through the winter. Cut the tansy when it is freshly opened, tie it in small bunches, and hang with heads down in a cool, shady place to dry. There you have it — beauty for the white winter months, a spot of color for a vase on the mantel.

*Trientalis borealis*, American starflower.

If you want to try to lure your deer with a special scent, the root of the starflower, *Trientalis borealis*, was known as a deer-hunting magic when thrown into the smoke of a fire — but what a pity to pull such a tiny little beauty from the ground!

*Trientalis latifolia*, starflower. (Photo by Henry W. Meyer.)

The American starflower grows mainly in the northeastern half of North America, but there are two other species that grow as far west as the Pacific coast. Only the American starflower has come to us with a reputation as a hunting lure.

The plant reaches only a few inches high, so it can easily be ignored entirely in the damp woods unless you know you are searching for the blossoms. It sends up stalks from a creeping underground root. At the top of each stalk such a few inches from the ground, leaves grow in a star-shaped whirl of tapered leaves. Backed by those leaves, one or two flowers or sometimes three pointed white flowers grow on slender stems, each small blossom only half an inch in diameter.

The whole starflower is such a delicate little thing that I hope that it will not be killed for its root by anybody today.

Other names for it are the chickweed wintergreen and maystar.

# 7.

# GOOD-LUCK CHARMS

There are hunters today who claim that they can get their quarry only if they use a certain gun. No other gun will do the job for them. This may be a bit of superstition, and they may even be the first to admit it, but they are not alone in feeling the need for magic.

Since the time of the caveman who needed meat for his family, hunters have wanted that extra bit of luck, of magic, to help them. Wild plants have had a full part in hunting folklore through the ages, and there are several still known to us as charms to bring good luck in hunting.

## *Acorus calamus*, drug sweetflag.

The drug sweetflag, *Acorus calamus*, was an easy hunting charm. It could have been created during the evening when dinner had been eaten and the sunset was dying in the west. Then, when the hunter had time on his hands, he sat quietly and wove a garland of the drug sweetflag leaves, flowers, and branchlets. The next day he wore it around his neck while he was hunting. Maybe it was its scent that attracted the deer. Maybe it was just magic. Hunters knew it had mystic powers. It was valued so highly that it took the place of money for some Indian tribes in bygone days.

The drug sweetflag grows from a stout creeping aromatic rootstalk along swamps and stream edges, and according to folklore that rootstalk had values ranging from mystic powers to power to cure various maladies.

American pioneers made a tea of it for colic and fever, and they chewed the rootstock for coughs, toothache, and colds. Chewing the dried root aided digestion and improved the appetite. You can also chew it like chewing gum just because you like it.

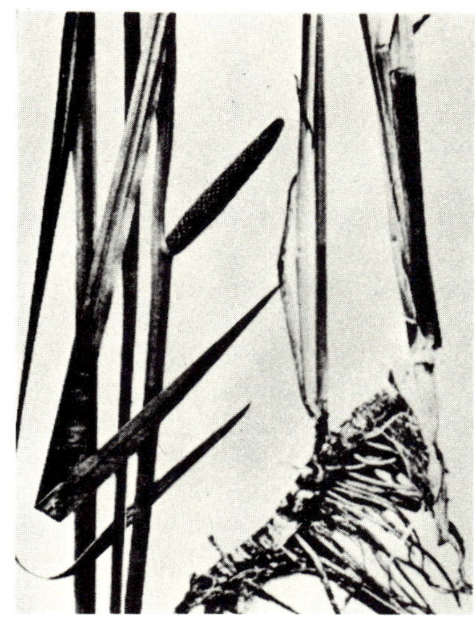

*Acorus calamus*, drug sweetflag. (Photo from *American Medicinal Plants of Commercial Importance*, by A.F. Sievers. U.S. Department of Agriculture.)

*Micromeria chamissonis*, yerba buena.

Some said it was fine for cramps in the stomach, or as a good physic. It was given as a stimulant to victims of typhoid fever or tuberculosis and even cooked with another plant for treatment of diabetes.

Root tea kept rattlesnakes away. Oil from the root is still used as an ingredient in perfumes. In Ceylon and India the powdered root is prescribed for worms in the body and used as an insecticide on infected plants.

A powerful plant indeed! Because of its wide reputation, it has of course gathered many common names. Know it as sweetflag, sweet cane, sweet grass, sweet myrtle, sweet rush, sweet sedge, sweet segg, sweetroot, cinnamon sedge, myrtle flag, myrtle grass, myrtle sedge, beewort, calamus root, or drug calamus.

Look for the tall, narrow leaves growing from the swamp, up to three feet high. In May to July you can observe the cylindrical spadix as further identification. Small, crowded flowers appear, yellowish in color, but mainly you will have to depend on those narrow, tall leaves and the thick rootstalk at their base. The sweet-scented leaves were once gathered to cover floors, too, so sample the smell of the leaves. The scent should be pleasing.

## *Micromeria chamissonis*, yerba buena.

*Yerba buena* is Spanish for "good grass." This native of the Pacific coast of North America smells good, and you can make a beverage from it — or a medicine. It is pretty, and it has a virtue that deer hunters should know. It is said that if you rub the fragrant leaves on your body when you are hunting deer, the animals cannot recognize your human odor. With your scent thus masked, you can creep silently up to the browsing buck and shoot your trophy.

Yerba buena is a delicately scented plant growing flat on the ground, with slender stems and rounded opposite leaves about an inch long. The flowers are small and white or purplish, opening from tubular bases. The crushed foliage gives the distinctive odor cherished by those who know it.

A tea was made by California Indians and settlers in the area. Besides being pleasant to drink, it was believed to be good to cool a fever or to settle the stomach. An extract made by crushing the leaves was prescribed for menstrual problems. As if that weren't enough, some people have accepted the yerba buena as a general tonic to cure almost anything within reason.

Find it growing in moist spots under shrubs and along creeks.

### *Napaea dioica*, glademallow.

The name *Napaea dioica* comes from the Greek meaning "nymph of the groves," which is a delightfully fanciful background for a plant that grows from four to seven feet high, with huge leaves up to a foot in diameter at the base of the stalk. It is a rather coarse, roughish plant, so any nymph that looked like the glademallow would have had to be a robust nymph, to say the least.

The Meskwaki Indians had no visions of fairy-tale nymphs dancing in their heads when they gathered the glademallow. The root was a fine hunting charm, and when they needed magic for hunting they relied on the glademallow.

The root of the plant was steeped to make a medicine for piles. The root fibers were treated in some way by women to make childbirth easy, and were treasured by them for other female troubles. Those root fibers also made a poultice to make old sores soft enough to heal or to reduce a swelling of the flesh.

There is only one species of *Napaea*, and that is the glademallow. Though the leaves are big, they are parted into many sections, and their lobes are cut and toothed. The flowers, in contrast, are small and appear in panicled corymbs when summer warms the earth.

### *Panax quinquefolium*, ginseng.

American ginseng root is one of the plants known for its hunting

*Panax quinquefolium*, ginseng.
(Photo by L.J. Prater. Courtesy of U.S. Forest Service.)

magic. In order to obtain the best results, you should check the shape of the root. It grows in fantastic shapes, and you should find a root that reminds you of the animal you want to bag for the dinner table. Just keep the root in your pocket — its magic will bring your animal to you.

Other names for the ginseng include sang, redberry, five-fingers, and man-root. Ginseng root has been part of folklore for centuries, and even today ginseng root is harvested for dozens of folk remedies, none of them scientifically upheld. Ginseng is said to cure impotence, indeed to be a powerful aphrodisiac. At one time the ginseng roots were combined with mica, gelatin, and snake meat to make a valued love charm, though the ginseng roots always had to be chosen with care. It is called man-root because of its tendency to sometimes develop leglike branches on its roots.

Though its medical value is scientifically acknowledged to be almost nothing, the ginseng root has been held in high esteem not only by some of the American Indians in the Midwest, but by the Chinese, who have valued it for many centuries, and by other peoples in many parts of the world who have experimented with it with much interest.

Ginseng is a medical miracle, if you would believe everything you are told. Dyspepsia, vomiting, nervous disorders, anemia, asthma, aches in the chest and stomach, colds, fever, colic, childbirth complications, depression, excessive thirst, exhaustion, eye weakness, headaches, heart failure, indigestion, insomnia, lack of appetite, menstrual disorders, nausea, nervous disorders, old age, weakness, rheumatism,

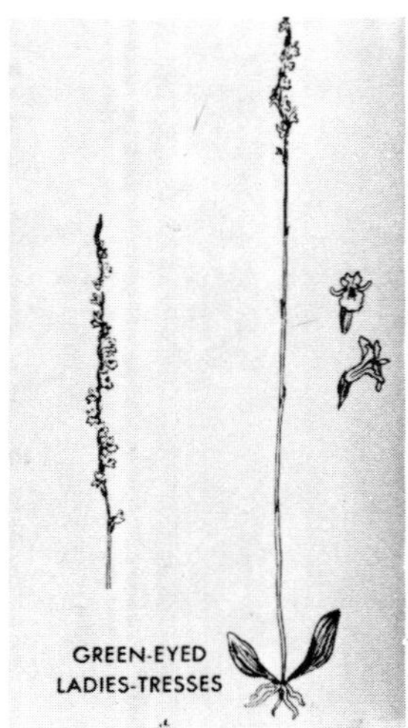


*Spiranthes gracilis*, slender ladies-tresses. (Photo from *Wild Flower Guide*, by Edgar T. Wherry, copyright 1948 by Doubleday & Company, Inc. Used by permission of Doubleday & Company, Inc.)

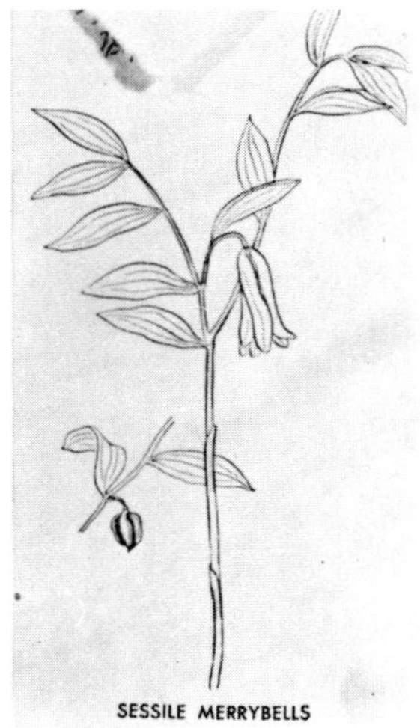


*Uvularia sessilifolia*, little merrybells. (Photo from *Wild Flower Guide*, by Edgar T. Wherry, copyright 1948 by Doubleday & Company, Inc. Used by permission of Doubleday & Company, Inc.)

and vascular cramps. Did I omit anything? Ginseng helps cure all these ailments, or so it's been said.

Tennessee mountain folks chewed the ginseng root for their nerves and swore that it was the best thing abroad for colic in a baby. To treat a child, boil the ginseng root first, then chop it so that it is easier to eat.

On top of all that, it is a seasoner to make other medicines more powerful.

You can well believe that ginseng root is a lucrative crop when it is grown and sold commercially. It is grown in America and in China, and Chinese roots are sold in America and American roots in China. There must be money in that kind of transaction.

## *Spiranthes gracilis*, slender ladies-tresses.

The slender ladies-tresses is one of the most delicate of flowers, though its leafless stalk can grow one to two feet high. The stalk grows from a few roundish leaves at its base — but if you look closely you will see the tiny flowers in a spiraled row at the top of that bare stalk. They are lovely even if they are so small. The blossoms are white, but they have an intense green central spot on the lip; this characteristic has given the plant another name, green-eyed ladies-tresses.

A couple of centuries ago the Ojibwa Indians gathered the root from this gem of a flower and used it as a hunting charm. We have no further instructions, so we do not know whether you burn the root, carry it on your person, chew it, or whatever, but we do know the Ojibwa believed in it.

The slender ladies-tresses is technically one of the Orchid genera, though it is a far cry from the orchid that is worn as a corsage. This species grows primarily in the eastern half of the United States and Canada, though related species are found as far west as the Rocky Mountains.

## *Uvularia sessilifolia*, little merrybells.

If you want only a buck deer in preference to a doe, look for the root of the little merrybells. I don't know what you do with that root, but it was known to the Wisconsin Indians as a fine hunting charm. Maybe you should just keep the root in your pocket.

The pale yellow blossoms of the little merrybells hang like small bells from the clean stems of plants only about a foot high. There are not many flowers on each plant. The leaves, which sprout directly from the primary stems without individual stems, are small and thick, gray underneath and lightly rough on their margins.

*U. sessilifolia* is a rather tidy-looking little plant. You will find it in the eastern half of America, though some plants may have crept slightly westward through the years.

Other common names are sessile-leaved bellwort, wild-oat, straw lilies, strawbell, bellwort, and sessile merrybells.

# 8.

# BOWS

If you want a really good bow and arrow, you should go to a sporting goods store and buy a commercially balanced bow and arrows with perfectly straight shafts.

However, if you should be stranded in the wilderness and need meat, it is possible to make a bow in somewhat the same manner as the Indian did when America was young. The long bow is one of the oldest weapons known to history, and though the crossbow was an improvement, the simpler long bow has been a military weapon through the centuries. Today there is a bow-and-arrow season for hunting big game in some sections of America.

Not being an authority on making bows myself, I turned to the Boy Scout's handbook for advice. Different cultures have made their bows with slightly differing points of balance. The handbook describes the British method of balance, quoting Alexander Pope's description of a well-balanced bow: "The perfect weapon is a trifle stiff at the center, and the lower limb is a shade stronger than the upper . . ."[1] The weight of the bow should be a trifle off center, the lower end being the heavier and the thick central portion being a few inches below absolute center. The ends of both the upper and lower parts of the stick are tapered to allow for the bending of the bow. The bow should be as long as the person using it is tall.

Grooves are carved at each end, strong and deep enough to hold the bowstring or leather thong. The upper end of the bowstring is fastened securely, but the lower end should have a timber hitch on the end so that the bowstring can be loosened when not in use.

There are many trees and shrubs known to folklore as proper woods

1. Quoted in Boy Scouts of America, *Revised Handbook for Boys*, New York: American News. Co., 1942, p. 529.

for the making of a bow, or a bowstring to go with it. Of the lot, surely one or two will be in your local forest lands, wherever you may live.

## *Apocynum androsaemifolium*, spreading dogbane.

A general description of this is in Chapter 2, "Sharpen Your Senses."

The fibers in the spreading dogbane are strong enough to make a bowstring if you plait several of those fine strands together. The fibers come from the outer bark of the small plant, and it must have taken a lot of them to make a bowstring as the plant itself is not very big.

Soak the stems, pound them to get the fibers from the stems, and remove any remaining pulp from the fibers. Braid the strands together, adding more as you progress until you have a long enough string for the length of your bow.

This fiber bowstring was constructed by the Menomini Indians of the midwestern states.

## *Carya ovata*, shagbark hickory.

Once you have your bowstring ready, look for the right shrubs or trees for your bow.

Shagbark hickory is one of the better-known hickory trees in America because of the sweet, edible nuts that the tree bears. If the shagbark grows in your area then it's the bow material for you. Not only were the branches of the shagbark hickory good for bows, but they also were excellent for anything around camp that needed a good strong stick.

The tree has a strong, tall trunk. Long gray strips of rather elastic bark seem to be loose on that trunk. The leaves grow in groups of five,

*Carya ovata*, shagbark hickory.

*Fraxinus nigra*, black ash. (Photo by Dirk R. Walters.)

two pairs opposite each other and a larger one at the tip of the twig.

The nuts are so good that anyone familiar with the shagbark hickory must surely gather the nuts. The tree has several familiar names such as walnut (though it is not a walnut), sweet walnut, white walnut, king-nut, upland hickory, white hickory, red-heart hickory, and shellbark.

Sap can be extracted from the tree to make sugar, and even chips of the inner bark can be sucked for the sweetness in them. Oil from the shagbark hickory was also once obtained for cooking purposes.

## *Fraxinus nigra*, black ash.

## *Fraxinus pennsylvanica*, red ash.

The black ash and the red ash were specifically mentioned for both bows and arrows, though other ashes may have been as good for the job. All ashes were once believed to hold mystic powers of various kinds, and that magic was supposed to be passed to the bows and arrows. Pipestems, snowshoe frames, sleds, basket splints, and even cradle boards were made from ash. It was strong, and it had that magic.

The common names of the ashes are all mixed up, so you will find the black ash also being called hoop ash, swamp ash, basket ash, and water ash, the latter because the tree likes to grow near water.

Besides making bows and arrows from the wood of the black ash, Indians added the inner bark as a seasoner for other medicines or took it for internal ailments of undetermined origin. White settlers boiled the bark to make a bitter tonic as an astringent and to control fever. Both the inner bark and the wood itself were valuable in making baskets.

The red ash is also known as green ash, blue ash, black ash, water ash, swamp ash, and river ash. The name red ash is the most appropriate. The buds are covered with reddish brown velvet, the twigs have red hairs, and under the leaves you will see more of those red hairs. Even the inner bark of the young branches is red, and you can eat that if you are hungry.

The red ash likes wet ground, and you will often find it in the low foothills of rolling country.

The inner bark was considered to be a tonic in the midlands of American. White frontiersmen said it was both astringent and something to take to keep a patient safe from a relapse of any disease. If you'd like to try eating red ash, scrape the soft cambium layer from the inner side of the rough bark. Cooked, it will be a dish to keep you from starving in the woods.

## *Juniperus occidentalis*, Sierra juniper.

If you happen to live on the West Coast near the Sierra Nevada mountain range, you may be able to find the Sierra juniper. The branches of this juniper were made into bows by primitive Indians before the whites came. In making bows from this tree, a craftsman would have to choose a branch carefully, then scrape the rough bark from it before it could be shaped to the proper weight and size.

This high-mountain tree is as often called western juniper as it is Sierra juniper, and both names plainly state where the tree is found. Its foliage is scalelike, covering the branchlets in pairs and in threes. The bark has cinnamon-brown, scaly plates, and the berries are the characteristic blue of juniper berries when ripe. The tree can grow twenty to sixty feet tall. Though the branches thicken to a broad crown, the winds of the high mountains can cause a short, twisted trunk at times.

The berries are edible, though too many of them may act as a diuretic. A juniper tea was made from the scaly needles and drunk for pleasure, in spite of the fact that stock can be harmed if they munch large quantities of the leaves.

## *Maclura pomifera*, osage-orange.

The osage-orange is so named because it has a fruit that looks rather like an orange, three to five inches in diameter and chartreuse to light gold in color. The two have absolutely no botanical relation.

*Maclura pomifera*, osage-orange. (Photo by Kate Jones.)

The fruit of the osage-orange is quite inedible, and its only use is to give a name to the tree.

The osage-orange has one great importance. It makes marvelous bows, pliant and strong. That trait is so well known that the tree itself is known as bow-wood in English and *bois d'arc* in French, the last name being corrupted to the American colloquialism "bodark."

The bark has a strong fiber somewhat like the flax fiber in its strength. The bark fiber is not claimed to be a bowstring fiber, but with the great preference that the American Indians had for the bow-wood in making bows, could it be that they were able to make the bowstring from the tree as well?

Various other names are tied to the appearance and the uses made of the tree. Because of its distinctive fruit, it is known as osage, osage apple, horse apple, wild orange, or mock orange. Because of its wide popularity as a hedge plant across America, it is known as hedge, hedge plant, or hedge apple. The yellow of its bark and roots give it the name of yellow wood.

It is a thorny tree that can grow fifty feet tall, but kept cropped it makes an impenetrable hedge, and for that reason it has been planted across America even though its native habitat is the south central part of the United States.

Its small flowers are pale yellowish green, nothing particularly remarkable. The leaves are ovate and pointed at the tips, from three to five inches long and from two to three inches wide. Their smooth margins and glossy, bright green color make osage-orange a beautiful tree that becomes even more bright when those leaves turn brilliant yellow in the autumn.

It has that wonderful elastic wood, pliable and firm, just right for making an Indian long bow, a policeman's club, or many other things. The wood is hard timber, hard enough for wagon rims and hubs, for house blocks, bridge pilings, telephone poles, railroad ties, and machinery parts such as pulley blocks. Mines and mills both find needs for it, and parquet flooring made from the wood will wear for years. Pioneers even whittled it into strong needles suitable for rough sewing.

Osage-orange is not grown commercially, but the wood is of such hardness that commercial industries have purchased the wood to make smoking pipes, artificial limbs, crutches, and fence posts. Game calls are made from the wood, too.

The wood is so resistant to rot and insect damage that it has acquired a reputation as an insect repellent. Housewives know this, and it is not unusual to hear of them putting hedge apples in corners of the kitchen cupboards to keep ants or cockroaches from attacking the cupboards. It is also believed that if you throw a few osage-oranges under the house, it will discourage termites from moving into the foundations.

The obviously yellow stem wood and root bark not only make a dye of that color, but they also contain pigments of green and brown as well. The color of the finished dye would depend on the treatment of the bark and the additives used with it.

The fruits seem to be worthless, yet when ripe and bruised they exude a milky, gluelike fluid. I have found no record of the sticky substance being used as a glue. The sap of the young wood and leaves is milky in appearance, too, and contains quite a bit of crude rubber.

This is a strange tree, but it remains the one tree or shrub known as bow-wood — the wood from which to make bows.

## *Prosopis chilensis*, common mesquite.

## *Prosopis glandulosa*, honey mesquite.

Common shrubs or small trees of the southwestern deserts are the honey mesquite and the common mesquite, which are sometimes confused with one another by both botanists and nonbotanists, though the two are slightly different.

They yield rather amazing sweet pods and seeds that have for centuries been a main source for desert Indians of food, housing, even clothing.

Both bows and arrows were made from mesquite wood, as were war clubs, spears, throwing clubs, and digging sticks. The bows were chosen with care from the strongest, most pliable branches and shaped to the needs of the hunter. When he finished his bow, he chose the smaller, straight branches to make his arrow shafts, then hardened bits of the mesquite wood in a fire and carved arrow points from them.

Another common name for the mesquite is algaroba, also spelled algarroba. The tree grows perhaps ten feet high as a shrub or as a crooked-branched tree up to twenty feet. Its thorns are a quarter of an inch to an inch long. Leaves are pinnate, with two or three dozen dainty, inch-long leaflets on each stem.

The flowers are small in the spring, greenish yellow in slender cylinders. When the flowers go to seed they leave long sweet pods about the size of common string beans, varying from three to eight inches in length. They have a slight curve but are flat and constricted between the inner seeds.

When the seed pods are ripe, the trees are heavily loaded with them, so heavily that the tree sometimes seems to be entirely covered, even though many of the pods have already dropped to the ground. Those beans are edible either raw or prepared in various ways.

The wood from the trunks and branches makes good poles for building desert homes as well as hunting equipment. Furniture can be made from mesquite wood. Charcoal made from mesquite burns long and slowly to warm a hogan.

The charcoal also makes a blue tattoo, as well as a black dye for fabrics; a blue dye comes from the leaves and pods.

A clear gum extracted from the trunks of the trees is an ingredient for a glue, a medicine, a black paint, and a hair dressing. You can even eat it if it is prepared carefully.

## *Taxus brevifolia*, Pacific yew.

Hunting bows were made from the pliable branches of the Pacific yew, and it is possible that bows could be made from other yews such as the *Taxus canadensis*, Canada yew, but I have found no confirmation of that.

The Pacific yew is a tree about twenty-five feet high on the Pacific coast. It is recognized by the two-toned needles with glossy dark tops and a deep yellow-green underneath the leaves. Instead of the cones that one usually associates with evergreen needles, the yew has red berries.

The yew has been a part of folklore for centuries, a symbol of long life and immortality. Because of the superstitions surrounding the tree, English churchyards and cemeteries often have a yew growing in them. Poets such as William Blake were prone to write such lines as ". . . mournful lean Despair brings me yew to deck my grave . . ."[2]

2. Blake, William, "My Silks and Fine Array," *Poems of William Blake*, p. 7.

*Prosopis chilensis*,
common mesquite (leaves).

*Taxus canadensis*, Canada yew.
(Photo by Robert Fielder.)

*Prosopis chilensis*, common mesquite (tree).

That was England, though.

In America, primitive Indians made a medicine of the yew. They mixed pieces of yew branches with leaves from the white cedar (*Chamaecyparis thyoides*) and the hemlock (*Tsuga spp.*), boiled them together, and had a remedy for rheumatism, numbness, and paralysis. They also took the branches and ground the roots of those three trees and boiled them together in a pot of water. They threw hot stones in the brew to create steam, then enclosed the sick person and the steam in a tent so that he had to inhale or absorb that steam. This is alarming to consider, since we know today that the yew's leaves, twigs, seeds, wood, and bark are all poisonous and should not be eaten under any circumstances.

In spite of the toxic qualities of the yew, its red berry can be eaten safely if you eat only the flesh of the berry, not the seed.

# 9.

# ARROWS

Some of the shrubs or trees known for making bows also have straight branches for arrows. These include the black ash, *Fraxinus nigra*; the red ash, *Fraxinus pennsylvanica*; the common mesquite, *Prosopis chilensis*; and the honey mesquite, *Prosopis glandulosa*. However, there are other plants that you may search for to make an arrow.

An arrow shaft must be straight and true. There are four parts to an arrow: the arrowhead, the shaft, the notch for the string, and the feathers (sometimes omitted), which are glued or tied near the end of the shaft to steady the flight of the arrow. The ancient rule of thumb to determine proper length for an arrow comes from an English tradition that the long bow should be as long as the archer was tall, and his arrow half that length.

It isn't easy to make good arrows, but for centuries they were made by hand, and they were accurate missiles when constructed properly. They can be deadly, as are the hunter's arrows of today, or they can be as harmless as the rubber-headed arrows for a child's toy bow.

*Acokanthera venenata*, true bushman's poison.

Though the *Acokanthera* species are not ordinarily listed in books dealing with American plants because they are native to South Africa, I find that a brochure issued by the County of Los Angeles, *Poisonous Plants of Southern California*, claims that *Acokanthera venenata* grows in that area.

It is actually the poison plant from which the African bushmen obtain the poison for the tips of their arrows. They have always done so, and will probably continue to tip their arrows with poison as long as their culture exists.

*Amelanchier spicata*, dwarf serviceberry.

*Acokanthera venenata*, true bushman's poison. (Photo from *Poisonous Plants of Southern California*. Courtesy of County of Los Angeles, Department of Arboreta and Botanic Gardens.)

*Amelanchier alnifolia*, saskatoon serviceberry. (Photo from *Trees and Shrubs of Lassen Volcanic National Park*, by Raymond L. Nelson. Loomis Museum Association, Lassen Volcanic National Park in cooperation with the National Park Service.)

The County of Los Angeles brochure says that the entire plant is toxic, but the wood is the source of the poison. From a worldwide plant encyclopedia I find that both the sap and the fruit are poisonous. It is possible that the bushmen dip their arrow points in the sap rather than make the entire arrow from the wood. The berries of the southern California plant have been eaten by peacocks in the County Arboretum, and the peacocks survived, so the berries may be less dangerous than the rest of the plant. Still, I would never eat one myself.

The *Acokanthera* spp. are evergreen shrubs with dark green leathery leaves. The flowers are white and fragrant, maturing to round black berries.

## *Amelanchier alnifolia*, saskatoon serviceberry.

Of course, before you start putting poison on the tips of your arrows you must have the arrows.

One shrub found in the western and northern states and in Canada is the saskatoon serviceberry, known for its edible berries as well as its suitability for arrow shafts. The branches are pliable and strong. If you pick a good straight one you have fine material for your arrow. Crees and Sioux along the Missouri River are known to have used the serviceberry branches in this manner.

The name saskatoon is traced to the original Cree Indian name. The Cree are a tribe of North American Indians formerly dwelling in Manitoba and Assiniboia between the Red River and Saskatchewan, which put them in Canada just north of North Dakota and Montana. That also spots where the saskatoon was growing. The *Amelanchier alnifolia* is also called Juneberry, serviceberry, shadbush, alderleaf sarvisberry, western serviceberry, western Juneberry, pigeonberry, shadblows and shadbushes, and sugar pear.

It grows farther south within the borders of the United States as well. There are thickets of them in the Black Hills, the Big Horn Mountains, and adjoining prairies and plains. It can be a shrub a foot high or a tree up to twelve feet high.

At least twenty-four different species of serviceberries grow in North America from Alaska to New Mexico. I knew the serviceberry in the Black Hills, where it grows so prolifically that it was not at all difficult to pick enough serviceberries for pies or jellies or whatever you might want; there the name is pronounced "sarvis-berry."

The various species vary from low bushes (dwarf serviceberry, *A. spicata*) to tall trees, but even the trees are easy to pick because of the flexibility of the branches. You can grab a branch heavy with berries and swing it down to a convenient height. It will bounce back to its usual height when you release it after you have gathered your harvest.

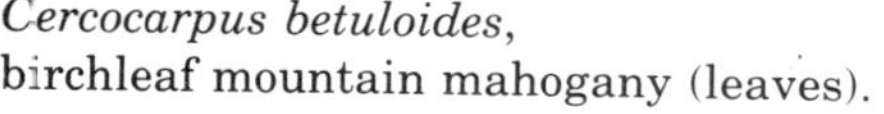

*Cercocarpus betuloides*,
birchleaf mountain mahogany (leaves).

*Cercocarpus betuloides*,
birchleaf mountain mahogany (tree).

The flowers in the spring are five narrow white petals with red or purple bracts at the base in some species. The berries are a dark purplish black, shaped like blueberries but larger and much darker. In autumn the leaves turn red, a blaze of color before the frost drops the leaves from the bushes.

The Latin name, *Amelanchier alnifolia*, refers to the fact that the leaves of this species remind one of alder leaves — roundish, blunt leaves toothed only near their summits.

## *Cercocarpus betuloides*, birchleaf mountain mahogany.

The birchleaf mountain mahogany has strong, stiff branches, just right for an arrow that will fly straight and true to its mark. California Indians knew this and used the branches not only for arrow shafts but also for fishing spears. Their women made digging sticks of its wood to secure edible bulbs and roots.

The birchleaf mountain mahogany is a shrub or small tree that prefers the dry mountainous regions of the western states. The simple alternate leaves are toothed at the upper edges, oval with a wedge-shaped base. The leaves are small, only a little over an inch long and less than a half inch wide. They are dark green above, but if you turn

*Chenopodium album*,
lambsquarters goosefoot.

them over you will see a paler green hairy underside that is not at first apparent.

The flowers are grouped one to three in a cluster. When the flowers mature, a dry fruit appears with a twisted soft plume reaching beyond the fruit. The tree has a scaly bark. Tea made from that bark was prescribed for colds on the West Coast, and the inner bark was stripped from the tree and boiled to make a purple dye.

## *Chenopodium album*, lambsquarters goosefoot.

The lambsquarters goosefoot is known far and wide for its excellent edible leaves and its black seeds, which are threshed as a food grain, but it has a reason for being in a book on hunting as well. Pawnee Indians of the central plains pressed the green juice from the leaves and stained their bows and arrows with it.

Why? When it is easy enough to lose a bright red arrow in long grass, why would they stain their bows and arrows the color of that grass? Perhaps, because they depended on their hunting equipment so completely, they wanted their arrows to be invisible to everyone except themselves, and they knew where they shot them.

Whatever the reason, lambsquarters were known to most of the primitive Indian races of America for their food value. Lambsquarters are tall, coarse plants growing sometimes eight feet tall, though the ones I saw in the Dakotas were only a couple of feet high. The leaves give the impression of being silvery green and somewhat mealy in texture. They are ovoid, strongly toothed or lobed. As the plants mature, red flowers climb in clustered compact heads along the stem.

They grow anywhere — waste places, dry hillsides, railroad embankments, flood plains — anywhere they can get a root hold. Because they are so well known, they have gathered a number of common names: goosefoot, pigweed, white goosefoot, wild spinach, frostblite, baconweed, muckweed, fat-hen, and calunay.

They are common weeds, and even sheep and cattle forage on them. If you want a salad, a potherb, or a dish of cooked greens, pick the leaves when they are young and tender. Let the plants mature to seed stage and gather all the seeds you can get. Grind them into a flour called pinole, which you can bake into bread. Ground more coarsely, the seeds can be boiled as a cereal.

Though lambsquarters may not be fashionable food plants at the present time, the seeds have been found preserved in burial caves dating back to the Iron Age, and such persistent plants may well become as popular again.

### *Corylus americana*, American hazelnut.

### *Corylus californica*, California filbert.

### *Corylus cornuta*, beaked filbert.

Though twenty-one species of filbert or hazelnut are acknowledged, only three are native to America. Those three are rather well distributed across the country, what with the American and beaked filberts growing in the eastern and central parts of the country and the California hazelnut taking over farther west. Whether you call them filberts or hazelnuts, you can find them coast to coast, from Canada south to Georgia.

Of course they have those edible nuts, but American Indians also knew them to provide straight, sure shafts for their arrows. This was true particularly of the California filbert, though some botanists admit that the California filbert and the beaked filbert are so very alike that it is hard to tell the difference except for the fact that the California has slightly larger nuts.

Not only arrows were fashioned from those straight, rigid sticks, the branches were good for drumsticks, too. The smaller twigs were tied in brushes or brooms, even woven into baskets.

Menomini Indians in the Midwest blended the inner bark of the

*Corylus californica*, California filbert.

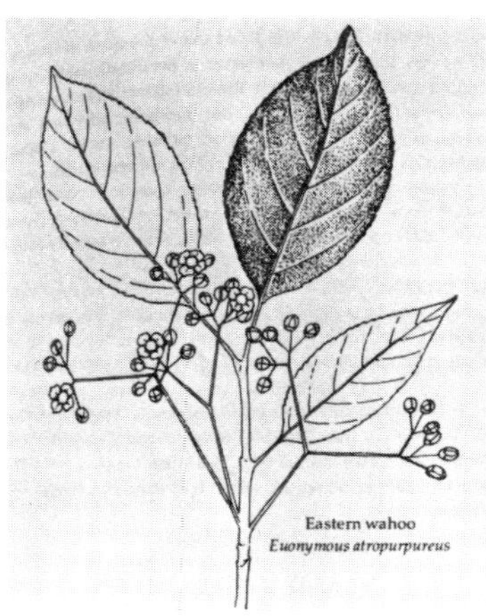


*Euonymous atropurpureus*, eastern wahoo. (Drawing by Juan C. Barberis from *Plant Medicine and Folklore*, by Mildred Fielder, copyright 1975. Used by permission of Winchester Press.)

hazelnut with other herbs to make a binder to cement the virtues of all the plants together. Some believed that if you ate the prickles on the burs of the husks, you could get rid of worms in the body.

The bark was boiled by Ojibwa Indians for a poultice to heal wounds. The seed hulls were known by the same Indians to set the black color of butternut dye.

These are shrubs or small trees. The leaves are hairy and elliptical in shape, varying from three to five inches long and from two to four inches wide. They have a suggestion of heart-shaped base and coarse margins, toothed in a jagged edge. The hazelnuts differ from other nuts in that the fruit or nut ripens within a leafy husk formed by clasping bracts.

Hazelnuts, like most nuts, are excellent eaten by themselves. I remember that as a child at Christmas, I always searched for the hazelnuts to eat first when I dumped my stocking treats into my lap. They have a delicately sweet taste that goes well in cookies, candies, and many desserts.

## *Euonymus atropurpureus*, eastern wahoo.

The eastern wahoo, often called burning brush or eastern burning brush, was named by the American Indians, referring to the arrows they made from the wahoo tree's fine straight branches. Their version was that if you say "wahoo" fast and vigorously it sounds like the noise an arrow makes when it is pulled back for shooting.

Whether this is true or not, it is a little tree with a lot of legends going for it. Sioux tribes along the western plains made a decoction of the inner bark that their women took for uterine trouble. The Omaha-Poncas called it the ghost walking stick, but I do not know the reason for this.

It is a shrub or small tree carrying a four-lobed red fruit, growing around twenty feet tall at the most. The leaves are ovate with pointed tips and finely toothed edges, and it has gray bark that is thin and scaly.

Indians in frontier Wisconsin made a solution for sore eyes from the inner bark and pounded the fresh trunk bark as a poultice for facial sores. The root bark was good for sore eyes, too, they believed. The stem bark was steeped by settlers in the area as a liver stimulant and as a drastic purge or a mild laxative, depending on the dosage.

Twentieth-century pharmaceutical handbooks mention the dried bark of the root as a medicine for the gall bladder and as a purge or a general tonic, though they caution that the action of the medicine is uncertain and irregular and that it should be taken only with thorough knowledge of what you are doing. Finally, oil from the seeds has been effective against worms in the body.

With all these values, the little eastern wahoo has many common names. In addition to burning brush and ghost walking stick, it has been called burning bush, spindle tree, Indian arrowwood, bursting-heart, strawberry-tree, strawberry bush, American spindle tree, bitter ash, and pegwood.

## *Holodiscus dumosus*, bush rockspiraea.

If you are hunting in the Rocky Mountains and need a new arrow, you might want the bush rockspiraea, *Holodiscus dumosus*, a shrub known for its straight branches, suitable for making arrows.

It would seem that this is primarily a mountain shrub in spite of the fact that one species on the Colorado front range is called ocean spray, even though it grows a long way from the ocean. It is also known as mountain spray and false meadowsweet besides the name of bush rockspiraea, which gives you some idea of its appearance.

The *Holodiscus dumosus* has pyramidal clusters of white flowers growing at the tips of its stems. The leaves are toothed with a silky appearance, lighter green underneath than on the upper surface. The Latin name comes from the Greek for "complete disk," which refers to the shape of the flowers. The sepals are united into a saucer-shaped

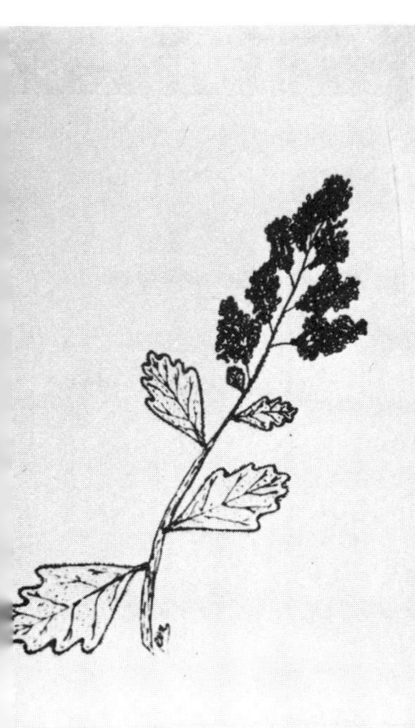

*Holodiscus microphyllus*, rockspirea. (Photo from *Trees and Shrubs of Lassen Volcanic National Park*, by Raymond L. Nelson. Loomis Museum Association, Lassen Volcanic National Park in cooperation with the National Park Service.)

*Larrea divaricata*, spreading creosote bush. (Photo by Henry W. Meyer.)

calyx, over which the five white petals flare. The alternate leaves, toothed or lobed on the ends, grow on stems one to ten feet high.

If you are familiar with the spiraea bushes planted as hedges in many areas, loaded with white blossoms during the season, you may recognize the bush rockspiraea by the similarity of its many white blossoms. Think of the name mountain spray, too, and keep your eyes open for them.

*Larrea divaricata*, spreading creosote bush.

*Larrea tridentata*, Coville creosote bush.

The creosote bush is also called the greasewood. To clear the air of misunderstandings immediately, there is another plant that bears the name greasewood. It is *Adenostema fasciculatum*, also called chamise, and has white blossoms, while the creosote bush has yellow blossoms. The chamise belongs more to the chaparral country, but the creosote bush likes the desert.

Indeed, the creosote bush has been called the most conspicuous shrub of the desert, and desert Indians found many values in it besides making arrows. They did not want the branches. They pulled the twigs from the plant because of a gummy substance that emerged when they did so. That gum was so gluey and strong that it held the arrow tips to the shafts with a tenacious grip, rather like the super glues of today.

The desert tribes also spread that gooey gum on their woven baskets to make them waterproof. They boiled the thick evergreen leaves to make a poultice for wounds, burns, and saddle sores. They drank tea made from the leaves for cramps or pains in the stomach, and even believed it would cure tuberculosis.

Creosote is a shrub three to ten feet high. The gray bark of the stems is banded with black. The small pointed leaves curve and shine as though they have been varnished. If you burn them, they smell like creosote. The yellow flowers bloom several times a year, beginning in April and May. Their five petals twist like the vanes of a windmill, and when the flowers mature they leave a round fruit that is white with silky hairs.

### *Oxydendrum arboreum*, sourwood.

If you should be in the eastern half of the United States in the middle of the summer and notice a tree that is blossoming with what appears to be lilies of the valley, you are probably looking at sourwood. The little white urn-shaped flowers are about the size and shape of lilies of the valley, and they cluster along one-sided racemes that dangle from the twigs on curving stems six or seven inches long — but this is a tree, and its blossoms are definitely not lilies of the valley.

The sourwood is one of the arrowwoods that gave their branches for arrows. Its gray bark is smooth and tinged with red in places; it also tends to be scaly and furrowed at the base of the tree. Taste it; it is like sour gum, hence the plant's name.

The tree can grow sixty feet tall under good conditions, but it is usually smaller. The reddish brown wood of the trunk and branches is heavy, hard, and rigid.

The leaves of the sourwood are elliptical, and though simple in shape they have finely toothed margins. These leaves grow five to seven inches long, and vary from one to three inches wide. In the fall when the lovely urn-shaped flowers have disappeared, the leaves turn scarlet to brighten the hillsides. The leaves too have a sour, rather lemony taste, and at times they have been used medically.

Other common names for the sourwood are sour gum, sorrel tree, and elk tree.

### *Pluchea sericea*, arrowweed pluchea.

The arrowweed pluchea is also called mock willow because, like the true willows, it grows on river-bottom lands, and because in some ways it resembles a willow. Mexicans call it *cachanilla*.

You will find it in California, Nevada, and Arizona, and east to Texas. Though it is a shrub, its common name arrowweed indicates what the southwestern Indians considered it to be. It sports a good straight stick for an arrow, but grows so prolifically in spots that it is almost a weed.

It is tall and slender like the willows, three to fifteen feet high. The leaves have a silvery sheen and a silky feeling and are alternate with smooth margins and tapering at both ends. They are not large, from a half inch to two inches long and seldom over a quarter of an inch wide. The flowers grow in clusters with many purplish disk-shaped flowers and no ray flowers. These blooms are surrounded by numerous bracts, the outer ones brown and tinged with purple but leathery in texture.

The straight, slender stems are what gives the pluchea its primary importance to man. Some farmers look on the plant as a pest because it

*Oxydendrum arboreum*, sourwood. (Photo from *American Medicinal Plants of Commercial Importance*, by A.F. Sievers. U.S. Department of Agriculture.)

FIGURE 100.—Sourwood (*Oxydendrum arboreum*)

*Pluchea sericea*, arrowweed pluchea. (Photo from *Weeds of California*, by W.W. Robbins, Margaret K. Bellue, and Walter S. Ball. Courtesy of California Department of Agriculture.)

has a tendency to make a thick, impenetrable canebrake. Some botanists suggest a bright side to this quality: The plants are so easily gathered that you can cut armfuls to spread on the ground as a mattress if you are camping near them. Southwestern Indians thatched their homes with those straight stems, but most of all they liked the stems because they made good arrow shafts.

*Rhamnus alnifolia*, alder buckthorn.

*Rhamnus californica*, California buckthorn.

*Rhamnus purshiana*, cascara buckthorn.

The woods that make good arrows include the branches of the *Rhamnus* species, of which there are some fifty-nine species mentioned in *Standardized Plant Names*. The three discussed here are perhaps the most widely known,

The cascara buckthorn is the official source of cascara sagrada, which is a known laxative, but both the California buckthorn and the alder buckthorn have bark with similar properties. That bark is boiled for a medicinal brew guaranteed to cure constipation when taken in proper quantity. The plants' berries are as efficient for the purpose. The name *cascara sagrada* comes from the Spanish for "sacred bark," a name originated by the Spanish who first colonized California in the wake of the Franciscan fathers. In fact, the *Rhamnus* species are so thoroughly connected with that laxative purpose that the suitability of their straight stems for arrow shafts is almost overlooked.

The alder buckthorn, *Rhamnus alnifolia*, is native to Iowa and the surrounding territory. The leaves, as the name suggests, are similar to those of the alder, oval and pointed, with the leaves roughly toothed or jagged. The flowers are greenish and grow in small clusters, maturing to berries repellent to taste. It likes the cold swamps of the northernmost states. Other names are alder-leaved buckthorn, dwarf alder, and dogwood.

The California buckthorn, *Rhamnus californica*, is also known as coffee berry, though both the berries and bark were made into laxative medicines. The leaves are evergreen, thin but leathery, oblong and minutely toothed. Not particularly large, they are from one to three inches long. This is a shrub or small tree, seldom over twenty feet high. The color of the berries is dark crimson to almost black; they grow from a quarter to half an inch in diameter. The laxative tea made from the bark is also considered to be a tonic of sorts, which might account for the name coffee berry.

*Rhamnus purshiana*, which is closely related to the California buckthorn, is the one sought for commercial purposes, though the other

Rhamnus californica, California buckthorn.

*Rhamnus purshiana*, cascara buckthorn.

species have the same qualities. The cascara bark and berries are a powerful laxative, but Indians on the Pacific coast separated the seeds from the berry pulp and ate them when foods were scarce, apparently without harm.

The cascara buckthorn grows along the coastal and inland portions of northern California, Oregon, Washington, and beyond those states into Canada. This is a larger tree than the others, sometimes reaching thirty feet high. The leaves are also larger, two to six inches long and up to a couple of inches wide, with rounded ends and toothed margins that have a tendency to curl under. The flowers are yellowish green, and the fruits are black when ripe.

That powerful bark is smooth and dark gray, and you will sometimes see it with cream-colored stripes.

*Viburnum dentatum*, arrowwood viburnum.

*Viburnum pauciflorum*, mooseberry viburnum.

*Viburnum pubescens*, downy viburnum.

All species of *Viburnum* are believed to have been used for making arrows, though only some, like these three, were so well known for the purpose that arrowwood became one of their common names. Known generally as viburnum or highbush cranberry, the different species,

*Virburnum dentatum*, arrowwood viburnum. (Photo by W.R. Van Dersal. Courtesy of U.S. Department of Agriculture.)

*Viburnum lantana*, wayfaring tree viburnum. (Photo by Dirk R. Walters.)

*Viburnum opulus*, snowball tree.

which are shrubs growing to eight feet tall, have their own common names as well.

Their leaves sometimes are maple-leaf shaped with three or four uneven lobes and jagged edges, or elliptical with fine-toothed margins. The white flowers are borne in clusters. The berries can vary in color according to the species and are avidly hunted for their food value, either raw or cooked. The viburnums grow from Alaska south through Canada and most of the northern section of the continental United States.

Their branches are slender and straight, lithe and tough, excellent arrow-shaft material.

*Viburnum dentatum*, also called southern arrowwood, grows in wet soil five to ten feet high in the central states. It has smooth ash-colored bark. The leaves are pale and broad, ovate with sharp-toothed leaves. The leaves are strongly feather-veined, with the veins prominently marked. The small fruit is bright blue.

You can find *Viburnum pauciflorum*, commonly called arrowwood or highbush cranberry, in moist thickets of the northern mountains. Though it is sometimes found in the Rocky Mountain National Park, it is seen more often in regions further north. The opposite leaves are both lobed and toothed, and when autumn turns them red they are a sight to see.

The small white flowers bloom in June. The Latin descriptive name of *pauciflorum* refers to the fact that this plant carries few blooms in comparison to some of the other *Viburnum* species. Often only two or three berries are in a cluster. The berries, which mature in August or September, are red and quite acid, but with so few blossoms to produce berries you will have a difficult time securing enough berries for eating.

The mooseberry viburnum was the one that Indians of the central and northern parts of the West prized for arrow wood.

In the states where it grows, *Viburnum pubescens* was often called downy arrowwood or downy-leaved arrowwood. From Wisconsin to South Dakota, and to the north and west, it clings to rocky ground as a low and straggling shrub. The leaves are ovate or oblong with pointed tips, and show only a few coarse teeth on the margins. Their distinguishing point is the soft and downy undersurface of the leaves and leaf stems. The feather veins are strongly marked. The white flowers bloom in spring or early summer, and the dark purple fruit is ripe in autumn.

# 10.

# BUTCHERING MATS

When you shoot big game, whether it be deer, elk, pronghorn antelope, or anything else, it is expedient to clean the animal immediately. Unfortunately, you may be in terrain that has undesirable plants growing on the ground, burs that cling to the least thing that touches them, gritty dirt that gets into the meat, bristly weeds that add nothing good to the animal being cleaned. You need a butchering mat.

There were at least two plants that were favored for mats by Indians and frontiersmen when big game was bagged. There must have been others, as luck is seldom so generous as to provide one of these two when you need it. There is one plant to be definitely rejected at butchering time — the grass called panic grass or switchgrass.

*Amorpha fruticosa*, indigobush amorpha.

The leaves of the indigobush amorpha were prized by hunters for spreading under meat that they were butchering. Some called the plant false indigo, water-string, or bastard indigo.

The indigobush amorpha is another of those big plants that can grow six feet tall along streambanks where it has plenty of water. It has long spikes of dark violet-purple flowers that appear during the middle of the summer, and its height makes it easy to find when you need something to spread on the ground to protect the meat of your kill. Its smooth stems bear small oval or oblong leaflets.

The indiogobush amorpha was not necessarily magic; it was just good sense. Medically, the indigobush amorpha was a colic cure, but whether the cure was made from the leaves or blossoms is hard to establish.

The leadplant, *Amorpha canescens*, closely resembles *A. fruticosa* but has soft, downy stems and leaves, while *A. fruticosa* is smooth.

*Amorpha canescens*, leadplant.

*Astragalus canadensis carolinianus*, Canada milkvetch.

*Astragalus canadensis carolinianus*, Canada milkvetch.

When a hunter finally shot his deer, buffalo, antelope, or elk, he was lucky if he was near a stand of the Canada milkvetch, *Astragalus canadensis carolinianus*. He yanked the leaves and stems from the plant to make a mat for his fresh meat. It was far better than trying to cut the meat on the bare ground. Everybody knew that.

This is the plant called little rattlepod. If you pick it toward the end of summer when it is mature and wave a branch gently, you will hear a sweet little rattling sound. It was gathered as a dance rattle by the Sioux tribes of the Great Plains, though the rattle is such a small sound that it must have taken at least twenty branches to make much music.

The little rattlepod grows from one to five feet high, but in the hill country where I found it the height was only one foot. The small flowers are yellowish to greenish, more creamy than anything else, with the flowers spreading in a relaxed cluster. The dried pod holding the rattling seed has a little tendril or hair extending from its tip, and the numerous narrow leaflets are typical *Astragalus* leaves.

Actually, the little rattlepod has several names, including the more generally accepted names of Canada milkvetch or Carolina milkvetch, plus Canadian milkvetch and Canadian rattleweed.

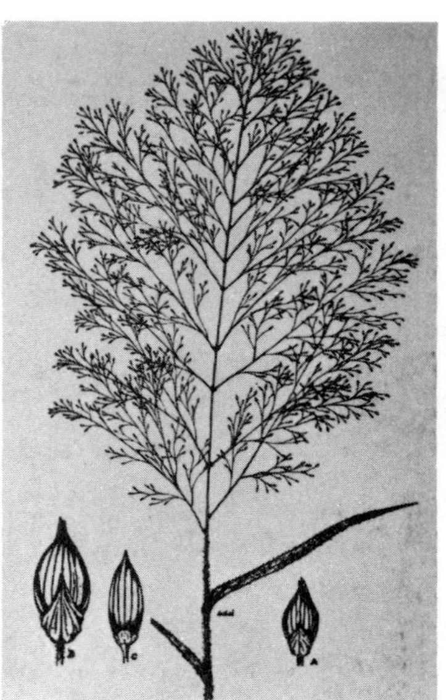

*Panicum capillare*, common witchgrass. (Photo from *Weeds of California*, by W.W. Robbins, Margaret K. Bellue, and Walter S. Ball. Courtesy of California Department of Agriculture.)

Its root was once boiled as a medicine to treat children's fevers.

*Panicum virgatum*, switchgrass.

Melvin R. Gilmore, who wrote of the plants gathered by Sioux Indians along the Missouri River for food, hunting, fishing, or any number of reasons, spoke of the switchgrass with emphasis. This is a grass to be avoided, he said, particularly when cutting buffalo meat shot on the prairie. The spikelets would stick to the meat and afterward would stick in the throats of the persons eating the meat.

What is this switchgrass, otherwise known as panic grass, witchgrass, wild red-top, thatch grass, wobsqua grass, or black-bent?

It grows almost everywhere across America, though doesn't quite reach the Pacific coast. You will find it in Canada, Mexico, even in Central America. A tall purplish-tinged grass from three to five feet high, it is an easy plant to recognize, and to avoid once you know its nuisance characteristic.

It grows on flood plains, in valleys, and in dry, rocky soil, flowering in late summer. The leaves are five millimeters wide (about a quarter of an inch), and its panicle varies in length from six inches to sixteen inches when its flowers have become those sharp, sticking spikelets.

Some 160 species of *Panicum* are known, generally characterized by a panicle of spikelets, with the seeds oval, roundly narrowed at the base, and sharply pointed at the top.

This is one to avoid as a butchering mat. Look to other plants for a smoother pad.

# SECTION 3

# FISHING

The mountainous areas of America have always been known for fine trout streams, but as population grew and the numbers of trout fishermen increased it became apparent that the trout streams would be fished out if something wasn't done. Almost a hundred years ago a few enterprising thinkers decided that fingerlings could be raised in a pond like cows in a pasture and then distributed to the free-running streams as soon as they grew big enough to be on their own. It was a fine idea but a difficult one to develop.

In 1887, when the first fish culturists began, it was not surprising that they should consider what to feed the trout. What was a trout's natural food? Someone suggested gnat larvae, and the hunt began. Gnats are small enough, however, to make their larvae tricky quarry indeed, and the culturists soon gave up that idea.

They experimented with grinding horsemeat and giant Norwegian fish, neither of which worked. Dried ant eggs were tossed into the pond, then maggots. The fish farmers caught dead insects and scattered them on the water, or threw in worms, which probably crawled right back into the mud. They ground crawfish (by hand of course), then salted meat, but the hand grinders were not fine enough, and to make a food small enough for the fingerlings it was necessary to grind the food twelve times, to the consistency of mush.

They soon tired of all that work and decided to try fly larvae, which they could raise in enclosed containers.

Unfortunately, all the junk they had been tossing into the pond polluted the water, and the little fish either contracted gill diseases or died of suffocation.

In 1893 the fish farmers tried grasshoppers and house flies, and again the fly larvae, which by 1908 were bringing ten cents a pound to anyone who would furnish it. Besides that, the Indianapolis State Fish Hatchery installed kerosene flares at night over the bass ponds to attract insects so that the fish could do their own catching.

Restaurants wanted more fish. Fishermen were catching more for the sheer sport of it. The culturists needed more ponds, more fingerlings, and more fish food, and again they looked at meat byproducts from the slaughterhouses. Electric grinders then being available, the fish farmers bought glandular parts of slaughtered animals until they were caught in a price war. Mink farmers and pet-food manufacturers were buying the meat byproducts, too. By 1934, when the Depression had forced a reduction in the slaughter of livestock, the price of packing-house products had doubled. Scrap fish was still available, so they bought that and ground it fine. Then a new idea caught their attention.

What about vegetables?

In 1938 the Cortland, New York, hatchery mixed a diet called the Cortland #6, made of skim milk, cottonseed meal, whitefish meal, wheat middlings (a byproduct of flour milling), and salt, mixed with hog spleen. It worked after a fashion, and in 1951 Cortland #6 was made into pellets for feeding—and the trout produced sterile eggs or became weak and died after being on the diet.

In 1961 the Cortland men finally managed to make a fish pellet that contained more vitamins and a variety of nutriments. It was a real breakthrough that worked. Brown trout lived on the diet and spawned eggs that survived and hatched with only a fifteen percent mortality rate. Since then scientific diets have been improved even more, so that trout can be raised satisfactorily in fish hatcheries today.

This recent search for an acceptable fish food is now history. Folklore tales take us even further back to the days when fishermen were trying their best to discover what fish liked to eat so that they could bring food home to their families. There were a few tricks that worked even then.

# 11.

# FISHING LINES AND NETS

A fishing line is a fishing line, and you are better equipped if you buy a good one at a sporting goods store today, but there are fibers that can be made into a fishing line of sorts for an emergency.

We found one plant (can you believe a seaweed?) which has a line ready for the harvesting. Who can kick about that?

Net fishing is legal today in some parts of America providing you have a permit for commercial fishing, or you can get a special permit for sports fishing in those states which allow net fishing.

Net fishing indicates that you must have a net, and many plants provide the material for making effective fishnets. The variety of such plants doubtless comes from the fact that different plants grow in various parts of America. Having a net, you can soak them in magical plants which will attract fish to your nets. So it was once believed, and they may be right.

*Agave americana*, century plant agave.

*Agave deserti*, agave.

*Agave utahensis nevadensis*, Utah agave.

If you live in the southwestern desert regions, you can look for the century plants or agaves for your fibers and find all you need for your fishnets. These are huge, thick-leaved plants, with leaves growing up to six feet high and flower stalks sometimes as high as forty feet.

You can call any of them agaves or century plants, but the individual species have picked up their own familiar names in most cases. For instance, the *Agave americana* is also called the common century plant, American aloe, maguey, or mescal. The *Agave deserti* is known

*Agave americana*, century plant agave.

*Agave deserti*, agave.

by only three names: agave, century plant, and mescal. The *Agave utahensis nevadensis*, Utah agave, also is called mescal.

All three species are used in similar ways for food, shelter, fibers, and for making the powerful drinks called pulque and mescal. However, remember that these are not the only agaves; there are some 300 species more or less, and they all like hot weather.

For making fishnet fibers, gather those rugged leaves. Dry them, beat them, and rub them with sticks until all but the strong internal fibers are gone. Alternately, soak fresh leaves until the pulp is rotted, then strip the fibers from the pulp. Cleaned of the last residue of soft leaf material, the fibers are ready to spin into a thread called ixtle, a cordage that was tied into fish netting and also filled many other needs. Shawls, blankets, carrying bags, cords, hairbrushes, combs, rope, bowstrings, baby hammocks, all were made from ixtle.

The century plants really shine as food. One of those enormous flower stalks provided enough food to feed a family for a week. A pit was dug in the sand and lined with rocks, and a fire was built over the rocks and allowed to burn to coals. The remains of the fire were raked from the hot rocks, and a layer of agave leaves or grass was laid over the hot ashes and rocks. Then the mescal heads were cut in pieces and placed over the leaves. A second cover of leaves was added, and earth or sand was banked over the whole thing. The century plant stalk was then left to bake for a day. Much of the baked agave was eaten imme-

*Agave utahensis nevadensis*, Utah agave.

diately, hot and juicy, but whatever remained was formed into cakes and dried for winter food.

For making pulque, you will need to bore a hole into the base of the agave. Push the end of a hollow gourd into the hole and suck on the other end until the gourd is full of the sugary water that flows through the plant. As much as two quarts of that sap can be extracted every day for several weeks if it is done properly. Store the sap, add fermented juice from a former batch, and let the mixture ferment until it is ready. If you have more energy you can distill the pulque and get the intoxicating beverage mescal.

In some areas the southwestern Indians made an equally acceptable sweet drink by boiling pieces of the dried agave cakes in water.

All in all, the century plant is a wonderful thing. If you see that plant with its mighty daggered leaves springing from the central trunk near the ground, if you see that imposing flower stalk reaching toward the sky in the spring, you know you are meeting an agave.

It is a sight worth remembering.

## *Apocynum cannabinum*, Indian hemp or hemp dogbane.

When native Americans wanted a fishing net, fairly often the plant they gathered was Indian hemp. The tough, stringy bark of the hemp dogbane was an important part of the plant, used not only for

*Apocynum cannabinum*, Indian hemp or hemp dogbane. (Drawing by Juan C. Barberis from *Plant Medicine and Folkore*, by Mildred Fielder, copyright 1975. Used by permission of Winchester Press.)

*Iris missouriensis*, Rocky Mountain iris.

making fishnets but also for general fiber needs as well. The bark was stripped and treated to separate the threads. While still damp, the fiber was plaited for bowstrings or for heavy ropes to tether horses; it was used whenever a strong cordage was needed.

The marijuana plant, *Cannabis sativa*, is also known as Indian hemp, but it belongs to a different family of plants. Marijuana is primarily known for its drug effects, but the hemp dogbane really had more value in its fibers. Both plants have similar medical properties, though the *Apocynum cannabinum* is a milder plant than the *Cannabis sativa*.

*Apocynum cannabinum* is listed in twentieth-century pharmaceutical handbooks as an emetic and an antiperiodic, but the caution is added that the dosage should be guarded as uncertain and irregular.

It was believed that if a piece of the root was thrown on a campfire, the smoke that resulted would ease a headache if inhaled. The root was simmered to make a tea that treated kidney trouble, dropsy (accumulation of liquid in the tissues), sore throats, heart trouble, or the ague —a name once given to intermittent fevers such as malarial fever or to the violent shivering accompanying chills and fever.

Other names for the *Apocynum cannabinum* are black hemp, black Indian hemp, Canadian hemp, American hemp, amy-root, bowmans root, bitterroot, Indian physic, rheumatism weed, milkweed, wild cotton, and Choctaw root.

This plant is a close relative of the *Apocynum androsaemifolium*, spreading rosy dogbane, which we reviewed in Chapter 7, "Good-luck Charms," but the hemp dogbane has white flowers in comparison to the pink flowers of its cousin. The flowers of the hemp dogbane grow in rather dense clusters at the ends of the stalks. Branches are smooth on a plant a couple of feet high. The flower of the spreading dogbane has a tube longer than its calyx, with the lobes turned back; the hemp dogbane shows a tube shorter than the calyx, and the lobes are erect.

The hemp dogbane is a dangerous plant if you eat it. Horses and cattle have been known to die if they eat only fifteen to thirty grams of its green leaves. Knowing that, I would hesitate to take it as a medicine, an aphrodisiac, or anything else. Use it for its fibers to make your fishnets. That is enough.

## *Iris missouriensis*, Rocky Mountain iris.

## *Iris tenax*, Oregon iris.

If you live in the great central part of America, you are more likely to find the wild iris for your fishnet fibers, though various kinds of wild iris grow from coast to coast. All iris can be used for their fibers in similar ways.

Two of these lovely blossoms were particularly admired for the purpose: the Rocky Mountain iris and the Oregon iris. Despite its name, the Rocky Mountain iris is not restricted to the Rockies by any means.

The *Iris missouriensis*, Rocky Mountain iris, has other familiar names: blue flag, western blueflag, fleur-de-lis, flag, flag-lily, snake-lily, and water-flag. This is the only species of iris indigenous to the western states, with the exception of the three Pacific coast states, where other species are found.

Only the outermost fiber of each blade was wanted. Once secured and stripped from the rest of its blade, this fiber formed ropes, snares, twine, and the fishnets very neatly.

The Oregon iris, *Iris tenax*, was one of the Pacific species most cherished for fishnets. The twine made from the leaf blades of this iris was known to be very durable and strong.

Any wild iris has long leaf blades growing from one to three feet high, depending on the climate and location. The blossoms are fairly large and beautiful, varying from three to four inches across. Most are a shade of blue, though there are other colors, such as the bronzy red of the copper iris, *Iris fulva*, found in the midland states and the South. So lovely are some of them that they have been called the poor man's orchid.

Make twine for your fishnets, yes, but do not eat any part of any of the irises. Their roots are known to be poisonous.

## *Nereocystis lutkeana*, ribbon kelp.

A fish line made from kelp?

In the Aleutian Islands off Alaska's coast, Eskimos made lines of the narrow stems that anchor this enormous brown seaweed to the sea floor. The *Nereocystis lutkeana* sends a stalk from its root thirty-five to three hundred feet to the surface, and there it produces an air vessel perhaps six feet long. From the air vessel fifty or more forked laminae or blades grow up to thirty feet long, brown and narrow like lengths of ribbon.

The Aleuts harvested the fine, small stems that anchor the brown seaweed, fastened a chunk of bait to the end of them, and used the contraption for deep sea fishing. This rig is definitely not for fly fishing, but we can hardly ignore its sheer ingenuity. And the Aleuts did catch fish.

This offshore seaweed was best collected during the summer months, because it was then in top condition, and also because only in the summer months were the harvesters not hampered by ice sheets.

Those long, thin stalks are also known to be edible, and are a major vegetable even today to those who know its value. The stalks are washed and peeled, then sliced like cucumbers or tomatoes and eaten raw. Cooked, they make excellent pickles.

The sea otter uses the air vessel floating on the surface as a bench or bed, and for that reason Russians call *N. lutkeana* the sea-otters' cabbage.

## *Photinia arbutifolia*, Christmas berry or toyon.

Off the coast of California just west of Oxnard, between Santa Barbara and Los Angeles, lie the Channel Islands. A federal reservation today, there was a time when Indians lived on the islands and made a living fishing the sea around them for food. Legend has it that the Channel Island Indians tanned their nets by boiling them in a solution of bark taken from the toyon or Christmas berry tree, thus making them stronger and better able to handle the ocean fish.

The toyon is still a prominent feature of California, up and down the coast. The first time I was fully aware of the beauty of the toyon in California was when I saw a small tree in the front yard of a Monterey home, loaded with bright red berries like a Christmas tree of holly. This appearance of the toyon has given it the names of Christmas berry and California holly.

The leaves are not as sharply edged as the true holly leaves, being oblong and rather narrow with slightly jagged edges and a pointed tip, but it is a mighty good substitute for the genuine Christmas holly and is even shipped east by florists at the holiday season.

It does not necessarily have to be a small tree, though it will grow as high as fifteen feet. I have seen it clipped for a glittering hedge; it can also remain only a shrub for years before it attains its full maturity. The berries are heavy from November to February on the West Coast, following clusters of white flowers earlier in the season.

There are eighteen species of *Photinia*, and some of them, like the *Photinia serrulata* or Chinese photinia, have the typical red berry, but the leaves have smoother edges than those of the Christmas berry.

Coastal Indians made a medicinal tea from the bark and leaves to cure stomachache or other unexplained pains. Inasmuch as toyon leaves may yield prussic acid, which is poisonous, it might be well to forget about that stomachache treatment.

The toyon has an edible berry, but do not eat it raw. It should be roasted, steamed, or boiled. Toyon cider has been made with some success.

*Photinia arbutifolia*,
Christmas berry or toyon.

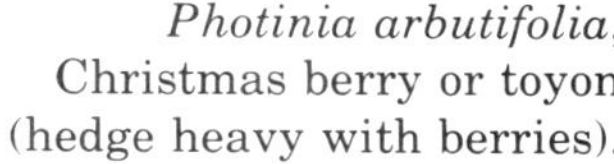

*Photinia arbutifolia*,
Christmas berry or toyon
(hedge heavy with berries).

## *Pseudotsuga taxifolia*, Douglas fir.

The stately Douglas fir that I described more fully in Chapter 6, "Smoke Scents," had great value in the lives of fishermen as well.

Dip nets are a convenient tool, and the poles that held those nets have been made of Douglas fir.

Salmon run in the rivers of the Northwest, and because of their tendency to return to the high-river spawning grounds at certain seasons, it is possible to catch the salmon by harpooning them instead of netting them. The Indian tribes of the Northwest knew that the straight wood of the Douglas fir was the wood to make those harpoon shafts. Having found a strong, straight branch for the main shaft, they tipped the harpoon with fore shafts made from the wood of one of the serviceberries, *Amelanchier* spp., found in that area.

## *Tilia americana*, American linden.

The American linden tree is also known as basswood, plus a dozen or more other common names such as whitewood, bast tree, black lime tree, American lin tree, American lime tree, beetree, daddynut tree, monkeynut tree, whistlewood, white lind, red basswood, yellow basswood, wickup, and linden tree.

Whatever you call it, the inner bark yields a fine fiber that was preferred for several needs in the primitive household, including fishnets. This is an eastern tree, but it extends a good third of the way westward across the country before it becomes scarce.

The American Indians along the Atlantic coast and the Great Lakes were doubtless the ones who first used the basswood for fishnets. They stripped the outer bark, then carefully removed the bast, or inner bark, which wrapped the trunk of the tree with tough fibers. Those fibers, soaked and separated, were tied into nets or woven into other items, such as mats, ropes, chair bottoms, baskets, and netting for snowshoes.

The young tender tips of sprouts and twigs were eaten both fresh and raw, but if it were later in the season the Indians did not eat parts of the basswood; instead, they gathered bark and twigs or seeds for medicines. The inner bark made a poultice to cause boils to open. The twigs were steeped for a tea that was drunk for lung troubles. Seeds were pounded for their oil, and dried flowers were gathered to make other medicines.

A tall, beautiful tree, it is a handsome shade tree. The large heart-shaped leaves are easy to identify, and the springtime flowers have a delicate perfume that may lure you to the tree as surely as the nets made from its fibers caught the fish.

*Tilia americana*, American linden. Photo from *Flora of South Dakota*, by William H. Over. Courtesy of ·versity of South Dakota Museum.)

*Urtica gracilis*, slim nettle.

*Urtica dioica*, bigsting nettle.

*Urtica gracilis*, slim nettle.

All nettles have a strong fiber in the bark of their stems, and both the bigsting nettle and the slim nettle are known in history as being important for that reason, though other nettles may well have been used, too.

If you really need an emergency fishing line, you can make one from nettle fiber. Pick the longest stems you can find, but if you value your comfort cut the stems with scissors or a knife and wear leather or plastic gloves when harvesting the stems. Hot water will quickly dispel the stinging properties of the leaves and stems, so strip the leaves from the stems and place the stems in a large kettle. Pour boiling water over them and let them soak for a few minutes. The stalks can then be lifted from the water and pounded to free the fiber from the bark.

Clean the released fiber as well as possible, then either twist or braid the fibers (adding more as you need to make the line long enough) and you will eventually have a fishing line.

The nettles have been described as weeds full of stings. The stinging mechanisms are not thorns but stiff, brittle hairs that are hollow and extend from bases filled with a fluid containing formic acid. When your skin touches the bristles, they release that formic acid, and you feel a stinging and itching sensation wherever you have touched the nettle. Rub the sting with the nettle leaf itself, that seems to help. If you see some dock (*Rumex* spp.) nearby, gather a few leaves, and rub the itching area briskly.

The nettles grow anywhere from a few inches to seven feet tall, but the bigsting nettle is generally only two or three feet high. The deeply cut leaves are somewhat heart-shaped at the base, oval and pointed on the ends. They are downy on the underside, opposite, and coarsely veined. When the small green flowers bloom later in the summer, they dangle between the leaves of the stalk, adding little beauty to the nettle.

The nettles have a real value for man in spite of their stinging ability. Gather the tender young leaves in the springtime, using a scissors and gloves, and drop them into boiling water to eat as greens. An old legend says that if you eat nettle soup in the springtime you will become beautiful, but whether you gain in beauty or not, you might do well to try eating them, because they are rich in protein and quite tasty.

Nettle twine has been known for centuries, and in some parts of the world fiber from the nettle is still gathered to make fabrics or paper. Sioux Indians made twine and cordage that was strong enough to hobble their horses and to weave into cloth for bags or clothing.

The roots of most nettles are known to have diuretic properties. Midwestern Indian tribes soaked the leaves in hot water to make a poultice for heat rash.

The leaves of the slim nettle have rounded bases with tapering points, the leaves long and shaped like lances. Generally speaking, the slim nettle has fewer stinging hairs than the common nettle, and is also known as the tall nettle, slender wild nettle, narrowleaf nettle, tall wild nettle, or narrowleaf nettle. The bigsting nettle is also called stinging nettle or common nettle.

### *Yucca baccata*, banana yucca or datil yucca.

### *Yucca schidigera*, Mohave yucca.

### *Yucca whipplei*, Whipple yucca.

If you can't find a century plant, you may be able to locate a yucca plant instead. Though there is a small yucca that grows on the Great Plains, the big yuccas of the southwestern deserts are the fiber plants that were of great value to the early Indians of that region.

Like the agaves, the yuccas have other common names than the ones listed above. The *Yucca baccata* is known not only as the datil yucca and banana yucca, but also as Spanish bayonet, soapweed, or datil. *Yucca schidigera* shared the name Spanish bayonet. *Yucca whipplei* was also known as chaparral yucca, Our Lord's candle, or quixote plant. All three were also known simply as yucca, soapweed, or beargrass.

The leaves of the yucca are much narrower than the thick agave leaves. On some yucca stalks they grow from one to two inches wide like strong grass leaves sprouting at intervals; on other yuccas they grow from a basal grouping. Because they are narrower, occasionally entire leaves were gathered as a fiber for some purposes, such as lashing together framework poles of houses. At other times the leaves were treated to obtain the thin twinelike fibers. The green leaves were soaked, pounded on a rock, and plunged into water from time to time to wash the softer tissues away, until finally nothing was left but the strong white stringlike fibers.

These fibers were needed for tying fishnets, or for making ropes, twine, hats, hairbrushes, shoes, mattresses, sandals, cords, baskets, woven cloth, mats, and paintbrushes.

The reason for the name soapweed was simply that the root was a kind of soap—an excellent soap for shampooing hair or for washing blankets. Pare the outer skin of a yucca root and cut it into cubes. Place those cubes in a cloth sack and add it to the hot water in your washing machine. It should do the job as well today as it did when Mexican

*Yucca baccata*, banana yucca or datil yucca.

*Yucca whipplei*, Whipple yucca.

women washed their clothes in the nearest river with soapweed root.

The flowers and fruit of the several yuccas were eaten but cooked in a simpler way than the roasting pit method used to prepare the century plant. Yucca stalks can be eaten raw, but they can also be peeled and boiled or roasted if you prefer.

The banana yucca has large pulpy fruits that are said to resemble bananas in flavor. You can slice that pulp to make a kind of pie, or you can cook the pulp to a paste, roll it in one-inch-thick sheets, and dry it for winter use. The dried pulp can be eaten as it is, or you can cook a piece of it in water to make a yucca beverage, or a syrup if made thicker.

The yucca is a tall plant. When it is in blossom you can see it shining in the sunlight from half a mile away and know that it is a yucca. It is not confined strictly to the desert. Whipple yucca is also found on the California coastal lands within a few miles of the ocean, though not on the beach lands themselves.

# 12.

# FISH BAITS

Once you have a fishing line or net, you need something to attract the fish. Legend has it that certain plant juices will coax the fish to your line. Just dip your net or fishing lure into the appropriate plant juice and wait for the action. Although some individual wild plants were excellent baits for fish, certain mixtures were considered even better.

### *Acorus calamus*, drug sweetflag.

A description of the drug sweetflag is found in Chapter 7, "Good-luck Charms."

A couple of centuries ago, or perhaps earlier, the Ojibwa Indians in what is now Wisconsin made a root tea from the drug sweetflag and had a magic to catch fish in their gill nets. The nets were soaked in sweetflag root tea. This fish lure was understood to be magic, though some chemical in the plants may have been the critical factor.

### *Aralia nudicaulis*, wild sarsaparilla.

The root of the wild sarsaparilla was steeped to make as strong a brew as possible, then fishnets were soaked in it to absorb the aromatic scent of the wild sarsaparilla. It attracted fish every time, or at least often enough to feed the family.

Naturally, such a fine root was believed to have medicinal properties as well. Pounded, it made a poultice for sores or boils. Pounded and then boiled for a beverage, it was a stimulant. It was taken to increase perspiration. It was believed to bring about a change for the better no matter what the ailment. It might cure a cough. It was even said to purify the blood of a pregnant woman.

This odd little plant doesn't grow very high, only about twelve inches at best, and it doesn't put out many leaves or blossoms, but it has a fine fragrant root that was wanted and is wanted to this day. One single long-stalked leaf is produced, with a flowering stalk from a very short stem. The top of the leaf stalk divides into three parts with each bearing five small leaflets from two to five inches long. The flowering stalk on its separate stem has three small flower umbels of greenish flowers. Later in the season those blossoms will have become purplish black berries.

Common names include false sarsaparilla, Virginian sarsaparilla, American sarsaparilla, small spikenard, rabbitroot, shotbush, and wild licorice, though the name wild licorice belongs more properly to quite a different plant.

## *Cuminum cyminum*, cumin.

A general description of the cumin is found in Chapter 4, "Small Animals."

To catch fish, crush cumin seeds to release the inner oils and rub the seed and oil on your lures, whether they be flies or deep-water lures. This should not only attract the fish to the bait, but should mask the odor of the fishermen's hands.

Cumin seed is also one of the ingredients in the Fish-bait Formula, described later in this chapter.

## *Daucus carota*, wild carrot or Queen Anne's Lace.

Carp like carrot, though I don't understand how they developed that taste, wild carrot not being particularly a creekbed plant.

*Carp* is a term applied to many fish of similar species but particularly to a big one that can grow to a couple of feet in length, the *Cyprinus carpio*. Since it really does eat vegetable matter as part of its natural diet, and since it does like carrot, it seems reasonable to suppose that if you ground some of the wild carrot root and pressed that pulp to obtain the juice, then dipped your standard lures in that carrot juice, you would have a tidbit to the fish's liking. As an alternative to that rather tedious job, you can boil a common garden carrot, cut it in small pieces, and fasten a piece over a fishhook — an old-fashioned carp bait that really works.

Our garden carrot, now indicated as *Daucus sativa*, is a direct descendant of the *Daucus carota* or wild carrot, also known as Queen Anne's Lace. Wild carrot is safe to eat, but it is likely to be tough and bitter.

Queen Anne's Lace grows from two to four feet tall, even up to

*Daucus carota*, wild carrot or Queen Anne's lace (blossom). (Photo by Maxine Fielder.)

*Daucus carota*, wild carrot or Queen Anne's lace. (Photo by Maxine Fielder.)

eight feet where it is well watered. It has pinnately compound leaves much like the garden carrot, lacy and fine. The flowers are in a compound umbel at the top of the stems, white or in rare instances pinkish, with a few central ones in the umbel possibly even a dark purple, but you will usually see it as all white.

Queen Anne's Lace has branched, bristly, hairy stems, and that hairiness extends somewhat to the graceful leaves as well. This is a common weed in many localities. You will find it in dry meadows, fields, or waste places along highways or elsewhere.

Do not confuse it with poison hemlock (*Conium maculatum*), which has purple streaks or spots on its stems and smells bad. Queen Anne's Lace has clean green stems and is pleasant to smell.

*Pimpinella anisum*, anise.

A general description of the anise is found in Chapter 4, "Small Animals," as part of the Smallage Root Bait recipe. Though anise grows in the southern parts of the United States either wild or cultivated, the commercial supply for America comes from Jamaica.

Anise seeds crushed into a sort of elixir have been a traditional lure to attract fish for many years. Alone, the anise can be rubbed on any ordinary lure to make it a more potent fish catcher. Whether it is the scent or the flavor that attracts is unknown, but the fact of its being in the water does not detract from its allure. Catfish in particular like oil of anise. Anise oil rubbed on a fisherman's hands will mask his human scent as well.

Anise seed is one of the ingredients in the Fish-bait Formula, described later in this chapter.

### *Rubus spp.*, blackberries, raspberries, dewberries.

Where blackberries are growing so close to a stream that some of the ripe berries fall into the water, fish in the stream may acquire a taste for the fruit. Put one on a fishhook and try it. This is true of any of the blackberries or related fruits. Some botanists insist that as many as 400 *Rubus* species exist in the United States alone, and their names range beyond the simple designation of blackberry or raspberry.

Other names for the berries are cloudberry thimbleberry, salmonberry, dewberry, eyeberry, blackcap, bake-apple, flymboy, wineberry, and even nagoonberry. The plants and delicious berries of all the members of the *Rubus* genus carry a strong family resemblance, so a general description of the blackberries should allow you to identify them.

Some have thorny or bristly stems; some do not. Some have black berries, while others are reddish or even amber colored. The blackberries are black, or maybe red. The raspberries are red, but there is a black raspberry, too. The whole situation is so completely confusing that you cannot really count on the color to identify the berry.

So how do you tell the difference between them? One point separates the blackberries from the raspberries: In the blackberries the

*Rubus ursinus vitifolius*, grapeleaf California dewberry (a California blackberry).

*Vaccinium* sp., blueberry. (Photo by Dirk R. Walters.)

fruit (characterized as juicy drupelets) adhere to the core when they are ripe; in the raspberries the drupelets separate from the core when ripe, so that they drop easily into your hand as you gather them and will drop on the ground if you delay picking them too long.

The *Rubus* spp. are bushes or vines with trailing or climbing stems, and the leaves of the different species resemble one another, with minor differences.

As for the berries themselves, some will be less desirable for the table than others, but all can be made into wines, cordials, and fruit beverages. They can be dropped into dessert puddings of one kind or another. They make excellent jams and jellies, or they can be eaten raw.

## *Vaccinium angustifolium*, lowbush blueberry.

## *Vaccinium laevifolium*, smoothleaf lowbush blueberry.

## *Vaccinium ovatum*, box blueberry.

Fish will nibble at blueberries that drop into streams, as they will at blackberries or any other berries conveniently near the water. The blueberries are about the size of salmon eggs, and therefore they can be easily slipped over a fishhook and dangled in front of any hungry fish. They might take this bait more quickly than you expect.

Though the blueberry may have a whitish haze on its skin, there is no doubt that its color is blue. The blueberries grow on low shrubs. They may have been more widely scattered a century ago, but the best places to look for them today are in the mountainous regions of the western states.

All of the sixty-five species of blueberries were sought by Indians and westering pioneers. They are good sweetened with sugar and eaten with cream, or dried for winter eating.

Both of the lowbush blueberries *V. angustifolium* and *V. laevifolium* have been erroneously called *V. pensylvanicum*, but to be really accurate you should give them their proper Latin names. The difference in their common names comes from the fact that the smoothleaf lowbush blueberry has a smoother leaf than does the lowbush blueberry. *Augustifolium* means "narrow-leaved," which the plant is, and *laevifolium* means "smooth-leaved."

Other names common to both include dwarf blueberry, sugar blueberry, early blueberry, strawberry-huckleberry, or sometimes grouseberry, bilberry, or huckleberry.

These two lowbush blueberries are practically interchangeable as far as their value to man is concerned. The ripe berries were dried to keep through the winter, then cooked again to make a sauce and eaten. A tea was made from the leaves that was believed to purify the blood, though actually what happened when our pioneers drank it was that they acquired a few vitamins that they needed to supplement their late-winter diet.

The box blueberry, *Vaccinium ovatum*, is also known as huckleberry on the West Coast, but it is as easily found in more eastern hills such as the Black Hills in South Dakota and Wyoming, or even farther east. It is a low shrub that grows in the higher altitudes, preferring moist, shaded slopes.

The Latin descriptive name *ovatum* indicates that the leaves are egg-shaped, with the broad end at the base of the leaf. The easiest way to differentiate among the *Vaccinium* species is to check their leaves.

The flowers of the box blueberry are pink and urn shaped, and the berry that develops is so dark a blue that it is nearly black. Sweet, juicy, and delicious, it is good in pies, jellies, and baked goods. Many of the common names given to the lowbush blueberries can as easily be given to the box blueberry, but the name given them makes no difference in how they taste.

## *Vitis* spp., wild grapes.

Any of the wild grapes growing across America may very well be growing near a stream, their vines hanging near enough to drop grapes into the water, and some of the larger fish may grab a grape if they see it dropping slowly through the water. If they like it, they will try again. Try one as a fish bait on your hook. Any wild grape will do.

Some 600 species of wild grapes thrive in tropical and temperate zones around the world. They are known widely for the jelly, jam, pies, sauces, and tarts made from them, and they are absolutely essential for the production of the world's vast supplies of wine, whether that wine is made in a home kitchen or by professional wine makers.

All wild grapes are vines that climb toward the sky on whatever they can find for support. The leaves vary in size and shape, but generally they are as broad as they are long, saw-toothed or lobed with deep indentations. The grapes can be various colors, ranging from blue and blue-black to white, red, amber, green, and black.

Everything on the grape vine is edible — fruit, leaves, young shoots, tendrils — but the root itself is not edible. Even the sap tapped from a vine will give you a sweet drink, but if you tap a stem you will have stopped its growth.

Familiar names of the wild grape are many and varied. Some of those names are Arizona grape, blue grape, bullace grape, bunch grape, bush grape, California grape, canyon grape, cat grape, chicken grape,

*Vitis* sp., wild grape.

*Zea mays*, corn (cultivated variety).

downy grape, dune grape, fox grape, frost grape, mountain grape, muscadine, mustang grape, New England grape, northern fox grape, pigeon grape, pinewood grape, plum grape, possum grape, post-oak grape, riverbank grape, riverside grape, rock grape, sand grape, scuppernong, silverleaf grape, skunk grape, small grape, southern fox grape, sugar grape, summer grape, sweet-scented grape, sweet winter grape, turkey grape, wild grape, and winter grape. Doubtless there are many other names, but these are a good sample.

## *Zea mays*, Indian corn.

Carp like corn, too, though corn grows in fields rather than in creekbeds. How do you explain that?

Crush some kernels of fresh corn to press the juice from them, then dip your lures in that juice and tease the carp where it lies waiting for a bite to eat. That's all. You can also slide two or three ripe corn kernels over the hook as if they were salmon eggs, and possibly you will have just as good luck.

Corn has been cultivated from aboriginal times. Descended from the simple corn first harvested by American Indians, today's corn exists in a thousand different varieties. It is intensively cultivated, but it once grew wild, so we may include it in our herbal lures along with the little wildling plants.

When the colonists landed, they learned the Indian name maize and called the plant by that name or by the name Indian corn. Both names have stuck to the species *Zea mays*, though hybridized varieties have improved the original in many ways.

Corn has a tall stalk, ranging from a few feet to perhaps eight feet tall in the commercial cornfields of Iowa or other midwestern agricultural states. The stem is terminated by clustered spikes of flowers, which most of us know as tassels. The ears of corn grow lower on the main stem, with the familiar corn silk extending beyond the end of the ear as it nestles in its green husks.

The corn silk is mentioned in pharmacy handbooks of this century as an ingredient in diuretic medicines or as a mild pain reliever, though I do not know how it was treated to be thus effective.

The leaves are long, roughly twelve to eighteen inches, and have parallel veins. Those long, narrow leaves and the tall stalks are often harvested after the ears of corn are removed from the stalks, then fed as fodder to cattle and horses.

## FISH-BAIT FORMULA

Various recipes appear from time to time for making a fish-bait formula guaranteed to bring home the limit of fish. They may have been very effective if the fish were there, or they may have been simply wishful thinking. You never know until you try them. Some of the ingredients included in this particular formula were certainly those known to be attractive to fish in their own right, notably the anise seed and the cumin seed; others were believed to attract animals as well.

The mixture includes lovage, fennel seed, cumin seed, coriander seed, and anise seed. Mix them together thoroughly in equal or nearly equal parts. Measure seven teaspoonfuls to a cup of hot water, cover, and let it barely simmer for one hour. Strain and bottle to use when the liquid is cold.

Either put a few drops on your bait when you are ready to fish or dip the lure into the liquid to increase the lure's power.

General descriptions of the anise, *Pimpinella anisum*; coriander, *Coriandrum sativum*; and cumin seed, *Cuminum cyminum* are found in Chapter 4, "Small Animals," in the section on Smallage Root Bait. Some additional information on anise and cumin is included earlier in this chapter. Fennel, *Foeniculum vulgare*, is discussed in Chapter 2, "Sharpen Your Senses." Lovage, *Levisticum officinale*, was covered in Chapter 5, "Big Game,"

Because the fish-bait formula calls for the seeds of the fennel, anise, cumin, and coriander, it seems reasonable to assume that seeds of lovage were used in the mixture rather than other parts of the plant.

## SMALLAGE ROOT BAIT

A general description of the smallage (wild celery) root bait is given in Chapter 4, "Small Animals." This bait includes wild celery, anise, fenugreek, and coriander seed.

To use the smallage bait for fish lures, dip your lures into the prepared liquid bait or drop a bit of it on the lure. The bait enhances the fish lure by scent and taste, even under water.

Though the anise all by itself has been used for fish bait, the mixture is highly favored by some fishermen.

# 13.

# FISH NARCOTICS

One of the saddest nature photographs I ever saw was of a controlled pond where trout fingerlings are raised outdoors at the Spearfish Fishery Center in the Black Hills of South Dakota. The photograph showed 100,000 trout fingerlings floating dead, belly up — every one killed by the carelessness of someone who had pulled the boards in the water inlet structure, thus cutting the water supply for the fingerlings. The concrete raceway had become their grave.

When I remember that mass murder, I cannot be very sympathetic toward the practice of dropping certain plants into a stilled pond in order to stun or stupefy the fish. According to folklore, there were several wild plants of considerable help to fishermen in days when they might not have been too squeamish about just how fish were caught.

Mashed bulbs, leaves, seeds, or whole plants were thrown into a fishpond, and a chemical released from the plant temporarily paralyzed the fish so that they floated on top of the water. Thus visible, the fish were picked up easily by the fishermen. This was not exactly magic, but there is no doubt that in a day when chemistry was hardly understood, it may have been classed as such.

I am not advocating such an action, you understand. I do not recommend it at all. Today you don't dare toss something in a pond to stupefy the fish — not if you want to keep out of trouble with the rangers — but I am reporting plant folklore, and this is part of it.

*Aesculus californica*, California buckeye.

Both the seeds and the leaves of the California buckeye tree, *Aesculus californica*, had the quality of stunning fish so that they could be harvested, though the seeds had to be unripe for the purpose and the leaves or young shoots were not quite as effective as other plants' but were better than nothing. One had to eat, and fish have always been so exasperatingly uncooperative.

However, do not eat any of the raw buckeye seeds, leaves, or any other part of the plant. They are known to be poisonous to man and should be left strictly alone. One wonders if the toxic principle is absorbed by the fish and passed on to the hungry humans when they eat the fish, but I do not know about this. Even the flowers are poisonous to bees, it is said.

In spite of the innate poison, California Indians gathered buckeye balls or seeds when the years were very dry and food was scarce. They leached them until they were dry pulp and then ate them. Sometimes they roasted the seeds to make them edible. To leach the seeds, the Indians first ground them, then washed them in water ten times to remove the poison. Finally, the seeds were dried thoroughly. When ground, the seeds yielded buckeye flour, which could be cooked with water into a kind of mush and then eaten. It had very little food value, but at least it kept them from starving to death. None of the Indians would eat the raw fruits, knowing them to be poisonous enough to kill.

California buckeye leaves were sometimes steeped for a medicinal tea to treat congested lungs, but it was a dangerous medicine. It was far safer to eschew the plant as food, and instead use the twigs as drills to start fires, an important function in the wilderness.

If you have a toothache, you can chew on bits of the bark and lodge a piece of bark in the cavity. It might relieve you, but it also might make you mighty sick. It would be far better to go to a dentist.

Although the California buckeye is also known as horse chestnut, it is not the common horse chestnut, *Aesculus hippocastanum*, which grows in the wild and on landscaped lawns across America. Both the common horse chestnut and the California buckeye are pretty trees, and are well worth planting in private landscaping if only for their blossoms. White candelabra of blooms appear all over the trees when spring is in the air.

## *Chlorogalum pomeridianum*, amole soapplant.

The mashed bulbs or roots of the amole soapplant were tossed into the fish pond. Presto! Fish!

The soapplant had various other virtues besides the chemical that stopped fish. The name amole soapplant, as well as soap root or simply soap plant, refers to the fact that the raw bulb reacted like soap and was considered to be a fine shampoo.

Cooked, that same bulb was quite edible and could be eaten like a

*Chlorogalum pomeridianum*, amole soapplant. (Photo by Henry W. Meyer.)

*Aesculus californica*, California buckeye (seeds and leaves).

*Aesculus californica*, California buckeye (tree).

potato. The juice of the plant resembled glue that could hold together the fibers of the outer bulb strongly enough to make brushes. The young stems and leaves were eaten fresh, but the old leaves, too tough to chew, were kept to wrap around foods while they were cooking as an emergency cooking pot.

The amole soapplant has a large underground bulb covered with dark brown fibers, but you will first notice its long narrow leaves. The flowered stems grow even higher than the leaves, sometimes as tall as five to eight feet, but the white flowers are very small.

This is primarily a west coast plant and is found from California to Oregon on dry, open hills and plains.

## *Eremocarpus setigerus*, turkey mullein.

Another plant used to catch fish in the same way is the turkey mullein, *Eremocarpus setigerus*. The leaves and broken stems did the job; they contained a poisonous substance said to be a narcotic. Stupefying fish seems to be the only practical worth of the turkey mullein.

The plant is a matlike growth hugging the ground with its gray leaves. Both the stems and thick leaves have a dense coating of forked, bristly, star-shaped hairs, and it is those hairs that do the mischief. Ordinarily animals avoid eating the turkey mullein, but if they are hungry enough and do eat it, hairballs may form in their digestive tracts, which can cause death.

Turkeys and turtledoves like the seeds, hence the name turkey mullein. The seeds do no harm to the birds.

## *Megarrhiza californica*, California bigroot or wild cucumber.

Primitive fishermen knew that one of the best plants to make fish float on top of the water long enough to catch them was the California bigroot, *Megarrhiza californica*, also familiarly known as wild cucumber because, with its bladdery pod, it resembles a wild cucumber. This bigroot has an enormous root, shaped something like a hassock and about that size, which guarantees that once it has started growing the bigroot is not going to be easy to eradicate. Some of the roots have weighed up to seventy pounds each.

Fishermen didn't want that enormous root. They picked the leaves, crushed them, and tossed them into the stream or pond. In a few minutes, there was dinner waiting to be scooped from the water. Not only did the leaves have a stunning effect on fish, but the seeds of the plant were taken for kidney disorders.

*M. californica* is a vine that wanders over the ground or climbs on whatever is available. Its leaves are thin, five to seven lobed and two to four inches wide, rough in texture. The flowers are small and white or greenish white; they mature to a dry bladdery fruit that is round and spiny, about two inches in diameter.

The bigroot is also known as man root or coyote vine. Eastern Indians called it the big Indian or man-in-the-ground. That they had a name for it indicates the plant grows in other areas beyond California, in spite of its accepted common name.

*Trichostema lanatum*, woolly bluecurls.

*Trichostema lanceolatum*, vinegar bluecurls.

Both the woolly bluecurls and vinegar bluecurls were mashed and tossed into a fishpond to stun the fish. They were known primarily on the West Coast.

*Eremocarpus setigerus*, turkey mullein. (Photo by Henry W. Meyer.)

*Megarrhiza californica*, California bigroot or wild cucumber.

Though the woolly bluecurls is named because of the bluish or purplish hairs on its calyx, the vinegar bluecurls also has hairy leaves. Both species have a strange blue blossom with long arched stamens, giving it the appearance of having stamens that are trying to escape for some reason.

The *Trichostema lanatum*, woolly bluecurls, also known as romero in the coastlands, is a shrub about three or four feet tall. The lance-shaped leaves have a definite fragrance, and the blue flowers climb up the stem with the leaves. A tea is made from the woolly bluecurls, an astringent that is applied to sores and ulcers. Both leaves and flowers combine for a cold drink to combat a cold. Aching teeth were once relieved by chewing those narrow leaves.

*Trichostema lanatum*, woolly bluecurls.

*Trichostema lanceolatum*, vinegar bluecurls. (Photo from *Weeds of California*, by W.W.Robbins, Margaret K. Bellue, and Walter S. Ball. Courtesy of California Department of Agriculture.)

The *Trichostema lanceolatum* was also called vinegar weed, camphor weed, or turpentine weed, because of the plant's distinctive odor. The strong scent can definitely remind you of vinegar, turpentine, or camphor if you get a good whiff. The Yuki and Concow Indians in California crushed the pungent leaves and young shoots and threw them in a pond to stupefy fish.

The vinegar bluecurls have very leafy stems from six to sixteen inches high, and the ashen gray, lance-shaped leaves are opposite and climb that stem at quite close intervals. Even their edges show the hairiness that covers the leaves. The flowers are blue in dense axillary clusters; bees seek them for their nectar.

The Indians of the West Coast boiled the leaves for a headache remedy when nothing else was handy. It must have some kind of sedative quality to have the reputation of being so effective in the fishpond.

## WHEN ALL ELSE FAILS . . .

One last plant cannot be ignored, because when all else fails you can still rely on the bog valerian to help you convince the world that you are a marvelous fisherman. All you need is one little plant, the bog valerian, *Valeriana uliginosa*.

The Menomini Indians believed that if they chewed the root of a bog valerian it gave them a great magic. Not only could they get all the fish they wanted, but they could win any argument that came up about their fishing or about anything else.

Think of the possibilities! To this very day, it would certainly aid some fishermen in spinning their tall tales. Or if you should inadvertently be trespassing on some private ground in your pursuit of a tempting trout, you could use the bog valerian's magic to persuade the owner that you were completely innocent, even that he should let you continue to fish until you caught that giant trout that you had been teasing with your best lure.

The genus *Valeriana* contains possibly a couple of hundred species, but when you go fishing what you really need is a root of the bog valerian, also called the swamp valerian or marsh valerian, in your creel. It is a rather small plant with opposite leaves, small clusters of flowers, and later a single hanging seed from each blossom. *Valeriana edulis*, edible valerian, is similar in appearance to bog valerian.

As you can tell from the name, this is the valerian that likes to grow in wet ground. All valerian roots are strongly scented, but it was the root of the bog valerian that was used medically. Tea from the roots was drunk for cramps and for disorders of the head, throat, and lungs. Pounded to a pulp, the root was a poultice for cuts and wounds, as well.

# SECTION 4

# HORSES

There is a certain freedom in riding horseback into mountain fastnesses, an independence of movement beyond the reach of those who travel by gas-powered vehicle. The horse can go anyplace, and because of that ability it has been a necessary part of life since long before the dawn of recorded history. Glenn Vernam, in his book *The Rawhide Years*, reminds us that men were riding horses twenty centuries before the birth of Christ, and probably earlier than that, though we have yet to find the evidence to prove it.

America first saw horses when Columbus brought ten mares and twenty-four stallions to the island of Santo Domingo in 1493. The first settlement in America was on that island east of Cuba, and Columbus' small herd was increased by enthusiastic stockmen for the explorers who followed Columbus.

Cortez and Villalobos took some of those horses to Mexico, and the Spanish paraphernalia of big-roweled spurs and rawhide riatas spread through Mexico and into the lands north of Mexico. Inevitably, some of those Spanish horses escaped into the wild or were stolen by Indians on the North American continent. Within generations the mustangs were running high and free across the plains or carrying Indian warriors on their backs. In a little over a century the horse had advanced across the face of America.

The horse has had other bloods mixed with it by this time, but those who know the horse and depend on its ability and durability know that it is an animal to be trusted and treasured.

Through the centuries men have tried to feed them, treat them with care, and give them medicine to keep them in top condition. The wild forage plants were man's mainstay in doing so.

# 14.

# FEEDING YOUR HORSE

Various early-day explorers mentioned the abundance of nutritious grasses that they found as they traveled westward. The historian Hiram Martin Chittenden, writing in 1935, stated that three main grasses were the chief fodders of the westward movement: grama grass, buffalo grass, and bluegrass, which he called bunch grass. Chittenden wrote of the American fur trade in the Far West many years after it was over.

Early-day eyewitnesses included the botanists John Bradbury, with his *Travels in the Interior of America, 1809–1811*, and H. M. Brackenridge, with his *Journal of a Voyage up the River Missouri, 1808*, published in 1816. Others followed those two. Maximilian, Prince of Wied, went up the Missouri River in 1833 and 1834 as an ethnologist, but he could not resist commenting on the plants of the region as well as the inhabitants.

First of all, because they had horses to feed, all these travelers noticed the grasses. Then they learned of the other wild plants that were of great value in keeping their horses fit and well fed.

*Bouteloua gracilis*, blue grama grass.

Grama grass was one of the three grasses particularly noted on the western plains as an excellent grazing food. It was widely distributed, and it so greatly resembled the buffalo grass of the prairies that it was often mistaken for buffalo grass. The two are not the same, though both carry dense one-sided spikes best described as brush-shaped. These spikes persist after the florets have fallen.

The spikelets are two-rowed on the flat axis of a one-sided spike, that is, each spike extends from one side of the stem only. Blue grama

*Bouteloua gracilis*, blue grama grass.

*Celtis occidentalis*, common hackberry. (Photo courtesy of U.S. Department of Agriculture.)

grass grows across the prairies into the foothills of the hills and mountains, and it has an abundance of food value. In dry years you may find it growing only ten inches high on the ranges, but a good season of rain can extend its height to twenty inches.

## *Buchloe dactyloides*, buffalo grass.

Much of the native prairie grass was the true buffalo grass, *Buchloe dactyloides*, which is still remembered as the best grass for grazing that a good horse could get. The land is plowed now in great squares of acreage. Most of the buffalo grass has disappeared with the large-scale cultivation of agricultural crops, but some of it remains to this day.

One botanist reports that in certain quarters the buffalo grass was known as early mesquite, but obviously it has no relationship to the mesquite bushes of the southwestern deserts. Generally speaking, buffalo grass is known as buffalo grass wherever you find it.

The buffalo grass is not tall, but it was the dominant forage when the West was new. Its stems grow only four to twelve inches high, depending on the rain or lack of it. Its most recognizable characteristic is the pair of dense spikes, one-sided and brush-shaped, which adorn the upper ends of the stems. There is sometimes a single stem, sometimes two or three. The buffalo grass has a shorter stem than the grama grass. Other than that, they do resemble each other considerably except in size.

Actually, the buffalo grass helped to settle the West. When it was still dominant on the plains, it grew in a continuous sod formation over large areas, so thick that buffalo-grass sod was what the settlers dug and stacked to build their sod houses. They needed a home to secure their claim on government lands, and with no trees to cut on the vast grasslands they used what was available.

*Celtis occidentalis*, common hackberry.

The inner bark taken from the trunk of the common hackberry tree was given to ponies with their regular feed as a conditioner, meant to build them to better health.

Pioneers also stripped the inner bark of the trunk to make an astringent, but whether that property provided a reason for feeding to the horses is not clear.

The hackberry grows as tall as an elm tree. It can be identified by its clumps of twigs in the upper branches, which are occasionally called witches' brooms. The light gray bark of the trunk has corky lumps.

Dark purple berries dangle singly on the twigs, and when those berries are ripe they are sweet to eat. Indian tribes ground them into meal and then cooked the meal as mush. There isn't a great deal of flesh over the seeds, but birds like them so well that it is difficult to pick enough for a meal unless you are right on the spot when the berries become ripe enough for gathering.

*Cuminum cyminum*, cumin.

A general description of the cumin is found in Chapter 4, "Small Animals."

One of the characteristics of the cumin seed is its ability to attract animals. Horses in particular will catch the scent of the cumin and move toward it in grazing. If your saddle pony has wandered away, try scattering cumin seed near enough to camp so that you can catch it when it returns for the seed. That method might be better than spending a couple of days searching for it.

If you have a horse who is nervous or generally intractable, you can soothe it with cumin seed. Rub the seeds in your hand and then pass that hand over its nose. It will become gentle and will follow you around. To really make a friend, place a few cumin seeds on sugar and give it to your pony to eat. It will be yours for life. Just keep a few of those seeds conveniently at hand.

*Hydrophyllum* sp., waterleaf.

*Hydrophyllum virginianum*, Virginia waterleaf.

The roots of the Virginia waterleaf were given to ponies to make them fat and glossy.

Sometimes called brook-flower, the Virginia waterleaf has leaves that are mottled as though they were water stained, which gives it the name of waterleaf. It likes moist woods and can be found by streams as well. The tiny flowers are only a third of an inch long, with color ranging from white to lavender to violet.

This plant also has astringent properties in the root, and therefore was believed to be a remedy for the flux. Nevertheless, the leaves are edible as greens if they are cooked.

The pinnate leaves of Virginia waterleaf have from five to seven main divisions, and globular clusters of flowers grow on a long stem.

*Lathyrus ochroleucus*, cream peavine.

*Lathyrus palustris*, marsh peavine.

*Lathyrus sativus*, grass peavine.

Two of the *Lathyrus* species, the cream peavine and the marsh peavine, were sought for horse feed, one to make a horse fat, the other to make it spirited, and both for forage.

Most people know what a garden sweet pea looks like. The blossoms of the *Lathyrus* species resemble the blossoms of the garden sweet pea, though they are smaller. The seeds of the wild peavines were eaten by many Indian tribes and by frontiersmen when the West was new, though the difficulty in finding enough for a regular source of food probably made the wild peas only an occasional dish for them. This is not, however, the garden pea by any means, our good garden peas being the species *Pisum sativum* and related *Pisum* species.

A Forest Service handbook notes that the cream-colored pea, *Lathyrus ochroleucus*, is a grazing plant, and that furthermore it is among the more palatable species. Besides the common names of cream peavine or cream-colored pea, this pretty white or creamy-yellowish flowered vine is called the sweet pea, pale vetchling, creamy vetchling, or cream-colored vetchling. Its ovate leaflets are about twice as long as they are wide. It is found in the pine forests or aspen thickets of hill country, trailing or climbing over neighboring brush.

Both whites and Indians ate the small green seeds when they found them, or sometimes roasted and ate the pods with the seeds still enclosed. This was a delicacy, not considered as a staple food.

The roots were eaten by Ojibwa Indians when food was not plentiful. White settlers made a medicine from the entire plant to cure stomach trouble, but they questioned the Indians' practice of feeding the cream peavine to their horses on the grounds that it was bad for the animals.

Eating the marsh peavine, *Lathyrus palustris*, was supposed to

*Lathyrus ochroleucus*, cream peavine.

make a horse fat and was also considered to be generally good for it medically, probably just as a conditioner or tonic.

It is a trailing vine with small rounded leaves and purple blossoms, much like the sweet peas of our gardens, though smaller in size. As its name implies, it grows on wet grounds, the wetter the better. The marsh peavine is also called marsh pea, marsh vetchling, sweet pea or wild sweet pea, or just the wild pea.

In recent years, it has been reported that certain species of *Lathyrus*, including *L. sativus* (grass peavine, vetchling, grass vetch), develop a poisonous principle in the mature plants, which cause a paralysis of the legs in men or horses who eat the entire plant or large quantities of the seeds. Young plants appear to be nontoxic, quite safe to eat.

The Latin descriptive name *sativus* means "cultivated," and so this plant was in southern Europe and parts of India. The seeds resemble green garden peas and have been eaten not only in southern Europe and India, but also in the United States when the land was newly developed and grocery stores were not as easily available as they are today. But one wonders. Should we feed such controversial plants to our favorite horses? Or should we buy them less exotic food, like oats?

### *Melilotus officinalis*, yellow sweetclover.

You can smell the fragrance of the yellow sweetclover if you are merely driving past a stand of it beside the highway, especially if the sun is high and the blossoms are fresh. Some say it smells like new-mown hay — and that is what it often is.

Ranchers have found that the yellow sweetclover is an excellent fodder for horses or cattle if it is well cured before it is fed to livestock. They even plant it for that purpose, though you will also find it growing wild in many places across America. If the sweetclover is improperly cured, left to rot on the ground or otherwise not dried, it can cause hemorrhaging in the animals. If treated properly, it is nutritious and palatable.

This is a delicate plant that can reach from three to six feet high, though the ones I've seen have usually been around three feet tall. The plant is branchy, with narrow cloverlike leaves and small yellow flowers growing in racemes at the tops of the branches. It smells so sweet that prairie Indians hung it in their homes for the fragrance.

Many years later, the dried leaves and flowering tops were listed in American pharmaceutical handbooks as being good for diarrhea, painful menstruation, and rheumatism.

In America it may be called the yellow melilot or yellow millet; the old English names are much more imaginative. They call it such names

*Melilotus officinalis*, yellow sweetclover.

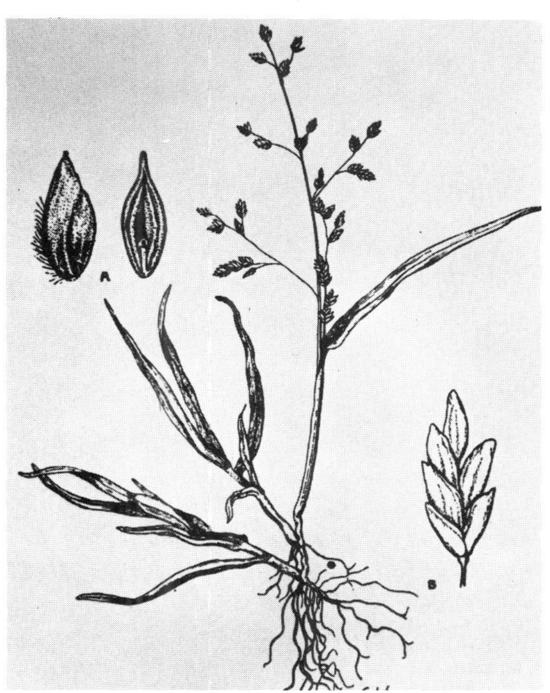


*Poa annua*, annual bluegrass. (Photo from *Weeds of California*, by W.W. Robbins, Margaret K. Bellue, and Walter S. Ball. Courtesy of California Department of Agriculture.)

as balsam-flowers, hart's-clover, king's-clover, king's crown, heart-wort, and plaster clover.

## *Poa arida*, plains bluegrass.

The *Poa* spp. are called bluegrass, bunch grass, or even meadow grass, depending on what botanist you consult and in what period he wrote. Our principal reference materials today list it as bluegrass, and on the Great Plains of America we are referring to the *Poa arida*, called plains bluegrass.

Hiram Chittenden, in his *American Fur Trade of the Far West*, mentioned this as bunch grass, *Poa* sp., and called it a rich, nutritious food for stock, the most widespread and important of the prairie grasses.

There are several common species, but they share a general appearance. The leaf blades are rather soft, extending approximately three inches from the stem. A terminal panicle holds spikelets with three to six flowerets that develop into naked grain heads.

Bunch grass is the name given to these bluegrasses because of their tendency to grow in clumps or tufts. The famous Kentucky bluegrass, *Poa pratensis*, has even lent its name to the horse-breeding lands of Kentucky, known as bluegrass country.

*Populus sargenti*, plains poplar or cottonwood.

When explorers and mountain men were moving slowly across the vast emptiness of the prairies, there may have been days on end when they saw nothing to eat. They learned that the cottonwood, beyond being a welcome shade tree under the burning sun of summer, also gave them food. They stripped the inner bark from that green tree, and they ate it raw as they found it. There were times when the grass was skimpy, too, and their horses whinnied in hunger. The men shared the inner bark with their horses, and the beasts ate it greedily.

I have always known this tree by the name cottonwood only, but it should actually be called the plains poplar, because that is what it is. It grows on the prairies and the plains of the western states, clinging closely to the little creeks that may dry as the summer sun bakes the prairies; they are often the only shade trees visible for miles. Other names are plains cottonwood and western cottonwood, but whatever you call it, the tree was important in the opening of the West.

Before the white men came to the prairies, the roaming Sioux had

*Populus sargenti*, plains poplar or cottonwood (leaves).

*Populus sargenti*, plains poplar or cottonwood (tree). (Photo by Della B. Vik.)

their own uses for the cottonwood. They knew that cottonwood bark made an excellent fuel for roasting clays to make war paints. The leaf buds were boiled for a yellow dye. Sioux children loved the big triangular leaves, folding them to make miniature tepees or toy moccasins for a stick doll, or even a whistle. I myself know how to hold a cottonwood leaf so that it will whistle when I blow on the tightly held edge.

It is a wonderful tree. Push a fresh green cottonwood twig into the moist ground along a sluggish creek. It will be a young tree when next you come back. Perhaps because it thrives so easily, the Sioux believed that the cottonwood had mystic properties of various kinds.

All poplars have the same edible qualities in their soft inner barks, but the explorers' histories seem to dwell on the plains poplar more than on the others as a source of emergency food.

# 15.

# MAKING YOUR STEED SPIRITED

It wasn't enough just to feed a horse. It isn't difficult to understand the need for a fast-running horse by the Indians who made their lightning raids on covered-wagon caravans crossing the plains, or by the white military men in the western wilderness who tried to keep order between redmen and whites during the Indian Wars.

Plants that were believed to give a horse an extra burst of speed were respected as good things. Several were known in the woods and on the prairies. Though they may not be used for that purpose today, they may contain certain chemicals that would give a horse extra energy for short periods of time.

*Lathyrus ochroleucus*, cream peavine.

The cream peavine was presented in Chapter 14, "Feeding Your Horse."

Some Wisconsin Indians fed the cream peavine to their horses to increase their running speed.

Later, white settlers called the plant a locoweed, though it is not a member of the genus *Astragalus*, which contains the plants generally known as locoweeds. Still, the whites refused to feed it to horses on the grounds that it was bad for them. If the peavine does contain a chemical that makes a horse slightly crazy, or loco, that might account for the increase in their running speed.

*Liatris punctata*, dotted gayfeather.

Dotted gayfeather root, *Liatris punctata*, was fed to horses in hot weather to make them spirited at a time when the heat had a tendency

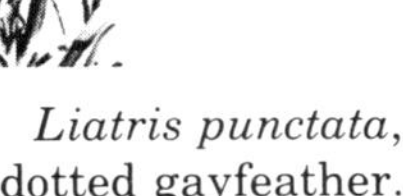

*Liatris punctata*,
dotted gayfeather.

*Lupinus* sp., lupine.

to make them lazy. Another name for this plant is dotted button-snakeroot, and some references give the name blazing-star to all the *Liatris* species.

Though some of the *Liatris* are said to grow several feet high, the ones I found in hill country were only about eighteen or twenty inches high at the most. Moreover, they were not so easy to find that one would hike into the woods to look for dotted gayfeather root if the weather was so hot that even the horses were lazy. There must be a better way to get those steeds moving.

The dotted gayfeather is fairly easy to spot from a distance. Its bright purple-violet blossom glows to announce its location. When you get close to it, the blossom has a feathery appearance.

The dotted gayfeather had its medicinal qualities in frontier days, and indeed it may still be wanted in remote areas for one ailment or another. It was steeped to make an infusion to be taken when the urine became bloody, or for general bladder trouble. The same liquid was said to be a cure for the itch when applied to the skin. Some people even thought that it might cure gonorrhea, but nothing has been proven on that score. Nevertheless, the white settlers believed it to be a good diuretic and of value in treating female diseases.

## *Lupinus* spp., lupines.

The pretty blue lupines have a reputation as being poisonous to cattle, but pioneer settlers and Indians offered them to their horses to make the ponies spirited and full of fire. They knew that the lupines should be fed only in small amounts and before the seeds matured. The lupine had an added value. It was believed that if a rider rubbed it on his hands, he would be aided in controlling his horse, spirited or not.

You may know the lupines as wild beans, blue pea, sundial, quakers-bonnets, or even Indian beans.

There are some 150 native American species of lupines, ranging in color from blue to purple to pink to white or yellow, depending on the species. The flower is small and something like a sweet pea in shape, but the leaves are the quickest means to differentiate lupines from other similar flowers. The leaves are narrow and grow palmately compound or, to put it simply, like the fingers on a hand spread wide open.

Some references say that the lupines are poisonous to sheep and cattle, particularly if the mature seeds and seedpods are eaten. In spite of this, gamebirds gobble them in great enjoyment and come to no harm.

Muenscher mentions in his *Poisonous Plants of the United States* that not all lupines are poisonous, but it is difficult for the average person (or even for a botanist) to tell which is poisonous and which is not. Perhaps the reason that it was safe to feed small amounts to a horse is because the toxic principle in lupines does not accumulate in the body but is quickly excreted by the kidneys unless too much of the stuff is eaten. You will know your horse is getting too much of them if it starts to breathe heavily and froth at the mouth. If that happens, watch out — it has been poisoned.

The lupines have very pretty wild blossoms and can be enjoyed for their beauty whether or not you want to coax your horse to eat them.

## *Sisyrinchium albidum*, blue-eyed grass.

Blue-eyed grass, *Sisyrinchium* spp., had similar folklore beliefs connected to it. If one gave blue-eyed grass to his pony, the story went, the animal would become sleek and vicious to the extent that it might bite those handling him, and if he did, the bite would be poisonous. The comforting part was that it would not bite its owner. If, however, you did happen to be bitten by a pony who had eaten the plant, the cure for the bite was some of the same blue-eyed grass placed on the bite as a poultice.

Blue-eyed grass was also a snake medicine so powerful that you needed only to carry a piece in your pocket to make snakes avoid you,

*Sisyrinchium* sp.,
blue-eyed grass.

or to keep some in the house to warn the unwelcome visitors away from the building.

Menomini Indians called the blue-eyed grass simply snake medicine, and another species known as prairie blue-eyed grass was just as effective in their eyes. I cannot find the exact Latin name of the prairie blue-eyed grass, unless they meant the common blue-eyed grass, *Sisyrinchium angustifolium.*

Meskwaki Indians boiled the blue-eyed grass to make a tea for hay fever in the summer, and they kept the tea for stomach cramps as well.

The plant is small but quite pretty. It looks like grass with a bit of a blue blossom unexpectedly growing at the top, where grass never has a bloom. Once you meet it, you will recognize it with no trouble.

The *Sisyrinchium albidum* is also called white blue-eyed grass by some botanists, but I have never seen a white blossom on the plant. Doubtless such a plant exists, since there are at least twenty *Sisyrinchium* species.

*Thalictrum dasycarpum*, meadowrue.

On forced marches, the meadowrue, *Thalictrum dasycarpum*, was fed to the horses as a stimulant to keep them going. The meadowrue was easy to see along the streams, a giant of a bush raising its tops

*Thalictrum dasycarpum*, meadowrue.

above most of the surrounding underbrush. On a forced march a rider had little time to look around for such luxuries as the waterleaf or even the hackberry tree, but often there was the meadowrue waiting near the watering spots.

The meadowrue grows from four to eight feet tall in moist meadows and thickets or near streambeds. If you have any idea of what you are seeking, you can see the plant from quite a distance. The flowers are quite small but have a purple tinge, which gives the plant the name of purple meadowrue, and its height accounts for its name of tall meadowrue.

The tops of the meadowrue were snipped as a love charm, to make a love medicine known for its ability to reconcile quarreling couples. Indians along the Missouri River stored the ripe fruits as perfume sachets in their clothing.

In the Dakota language meadowrue was called *wazimna*, which meant "pine-smell." The Omaha-Ponca Indians knew it as *nisude-hi*, which translated to "flute-plant," a name coming from the fact that the hollow stems were coveted by Indian children as toy flutes.

There was definitely a chemical property in the meadowrue. The juice of the meadowrue was smoothed on the head as a cure for headaches. A root tea was believed to reduce fevers. White settlers recognized the meadowrue as a bitter tonic, a stimulant, and an antiperiodic (a medicine used to treat recurring illnesses, such as malaria).

# 16.

# DOCTORING YOUR HORSE

In spite of your best care, your horse may get sick at times — with distemper, worms, lung troubles — or it may develop saddle sores from improperly fastened gear.

Just as there were hundreds of plants that were once believed to be medicine for human beings, so certain wild plants of the prairies and hills were gathered to cure sick or sore horses. A good horse is worth doctoring, and some of those early medicines might still be worth a try.

## *Artemisia ludoviciana*, Louisiana sagebrush.

A general description of the Louisiana sagebrush, also called lobed cudweed, sagebrush, white sage, or western mugwort, is found in Chapter 1, "Subdue Those Insects."

Among the plants remembered as being of value when a horse was sick with distemper is the Louisiana sagebrush. A campfire was built, and the sagebrush was allowed to smolder in the glowing coals. Then the horse was brought near the fire. By using blankets to form a tent over horse and fire or by other means, the animal was forced to breathe the smoke. Since horses are leery of fire at any time, this must not have been the easiest way to treat the disease.

## *Echinacea angustifolia*, blacksamson echinacea

Another distemper medicine was the powerful *Echinacea angustifolia* or blacksamson echinacea, known widely as the purple coneflower.

Frontiersmen used the purple coneflower to treat horse distemper in the same manner as they did the Louisiana sagebrush — by forcing

*Echinacea angustifolia*, blacksamson echinacea or purple coneflower.

the animal to breathe smoke from a campfire in which purple coneflower plants had been placed.

Regardless of the efficacy of the distemper remedy, purple coneflower cannot be dismissed lightly. It was a powerful medicine, and could be the same today.

There are four *Echinacea* species known, but all are listed together under the common name of purple coneflower. The *Echinacea angustifolia*, blacksamson echinacea, has picked up a few other common names: comb plant, narrow-leaved comb plant, pink coneflower, hedgehog coneflower, pale purple coneflower, Sampson root, niggerhead, narrow-leaved purple coneflower, and widow's comb.

Modern pharmaceutical handbooks state that the purple coneflower contains an acrid resin and a minute amount of an alkaloid that has a toxic effect on man much as strychnine or morphine does. Therein might lie its power, since morphine is a pain killer.

This was the plant once peddled around the country by itinerant quack doctors in pioneer days under the name of Black Sampson Pain Killer, a title that uses one of the plant's accepted common names. Long before the peddlers wandered the back country, Indians of the Missouri River basin knew its value. Their medicine men guarded the secret carefully because of the wonderment caused by the plant's seemingly magical powers.

The medicine men knew that purple coneflower could be added to a steam bath to make the hot steam more endurable. The juice of the plant would heal burns and even prevent them, so jugglers bathed their hands and arms in the pink coneflower juice. Having done that, they could take a piece of meat from a kettle of boiling water with their fingers without suffering pain, or they could rinse their mouths with the juice and then place a live coal in their mouths and not feel it.

Either action conferred prestige, and after having performed such wonders, a medicine man would no doubt have his people well under his control.

With that bit of pain-killing alkaloid in the plant, naturally it became popular for other medical needs. Snakebites or the bites of rabid animals were treated with the juice of the plant. Even gangrenous wounds were exposed to the plant for healing. Headaches eased when the sufferer sat with his head in the smudge of a campfire that had purple coneflower in it.

Toothache? Chew a bit of the stem or root.

Glands swollen because of mumps or other maladies? The purple coneflower juice would help.

Stomach cramps and fits also responded to purple coneflower medicine. White pioneers took the Black Sampson Pain Killer to increase perspiration in a patient with a fever, or to promote the flow of saliva if that was needed. It would make anything better, they believed. Even syphilis was given a dose of purple coneflower. Eczema and ulcers quailed before the stuff.

Purple coneflower is a mighty blossom if all the qualities attributed to it in folklore have any basis in fact. It is not a big plant, seldom growing much over a foot or two tall, and its pink blossom is just what it is called — a coneflower. The long lance-shaped leaves are rather rough with hairs, but what marvelous magic they have!

### *Fraxinus americana*, white ash.

As horse medicine, the white ash, *Fraxinus americana*, has come to us only as a treatment for unspecified ailments., but parts of the ash trees were used for just about anything that the settlers and the Indians could think of: medicine, food, fibers, lumber, magic, a man's perfume, whatever was needed. It is not surprising that the white ash tree was also considered beneficial to their horses.

Scottish mothers fed infants on the sap of any ash tree to make their babies immune to snakes. To add to the charm, the rockers of cradles were made of ash so that a serpent could not cross the rocker and slither into the crib.

An aura of mysticism remains with the ash trees beyond any pow-

*Fraxinus americana*, white ash.
(Photo by E.S. Shipp. Courtesy of U.S. Forest Service.)

ers to hinder snakes or help horses. If the plains Indians wanted pipestems with a little extra magic, they constructed them of ash. If an especially powerful bow was needed, it had to be of ash. If the arrow shafts were to fly true and straight, it took the magic of the ash to make the arrows. Snowshoe frames, sleds, basket splints, and cradle boards were all better for being made of ash.

Of course the ash had many medical qualities. How could it help but have them when it added a magic elixir to everything it touched?

A bark infusion cured sores and skin itching, lice on the scalp, internal ailments of any kind, and constipation. It was also used as a general tonic or as a seasoner for other medicines.

Tennessee mountain folks broke a stick from any ash tree, put it in a fire until the sap bubbled from the end, and then put a drop of that

*Fraxinus lanceolata*, green ash (tree).

*Fraxinus lanceolata*, green ash (leaves).

hot sap into a child's ear to cure an earache. They swore by the treatment, but today it sounds like a form of torture.

Whites on the frontier borrowed many of the Indians' beliefs on the medicinal uses of the ash and added a few of their own. It was an astringent, a preventive of intermittent fevers, and a bitter tonic. Even as late as 1917, pharmaceutical books listed the ash for those three reasons.

Twenty species of ash trees exist in America, of which the white ash of the eastern half of the United States is the best known. However, there are four ashes that are fairly close in appearance and characteristics, so much so that they share many of the same common names. They are *Fraxinus americana*, white ash, also called ash, American white ash, and cane ash; *Fraxinus lanceolata*, the green ash, but sometimes confused with red ash; *Fraxinus nigra*, black ash, also called the hoop ash, swamp ash, water ash, and basket ash; *Fraxinus pennsylvanica*, the red ash, also called green ash, blue ash, black ash, water ash, swamp ash, or river ash.

*Glycyrrhiza lepidota*, American licorice.

*Grindelia squarrosa*, curlycup gumweed.

## *Glycyrrhiza lepidota*, American licorice.

To ease a sore back on your favorite horse, chew the leaves of some American or wild licorice, *Glycyrrhiza lepidota*, to a paste, then apply the chewed leaves to its hide as a poultice.

The American licorice has other medical qualities, too, so perhaps its value in healing saddle sores was not exaggerated. Pioneers chewed the wild licorice root for toothaches, holding the wad of root in the mouth until the tooth felt better. For earache the leaves were steeped, then drops of the tepid liquid were placed in the ear. If a child had a fever, his mother boiled the root of wild licorice, not the leaves, and gave the sick child a spoonful at intervals to bring the fever down.

*G. lepidota* is a pretty plant, with clean small green leaves and racemes of white blossoms. The white flowers of the licorice stand from one to four feet above the ground. If you hold the plant close to your nose and sniff, you can detect the scent of licorice.

## *Grindelia squarrosa*, curlycup gumweed.

When saddle galls or sores appeared, frontiersmen sometimes searched for the curlycup gumweed or stickyhead, *Grindelia squarrosa*. The recipe called for boiling the tops and leaves. After the liquid cooled it was a wash for the animal's sore back, to be repeated as often as necessary.

Gum plant, broad-leaved gum plant, and scaly grindelia are other names for this one, but we like the name stickyhead best because it is quite descriptive. A child can pull the blossom from the plant's stem and stick it squarely on his fingertips, or five blossoms on five fingertips, and the blossoms will stick like glue. The flowers are yellow, about an inch across, rather flat in appearance. The leaves are alternate and usually spiny-toothed, framing a blossom that appears in late summer or early autumn.

Gumweed is also known as a cure for the itch of poison ivy, and in fact fluid of Grindelia was sold in drugstores for that reason, only a few years ago. It may still be available.

White settlers made a brew of the tops and leaves, which they administered to small children for the colic and to their elders for consumption. Bronchitis and asthma were believed to be made better by the taking of gumweed tea, as well. A 1917 pharmaceutical handbook mentioned that the dried leaves and flowering tops of the stickyhead made a mild stomach medicine and an expectorant.

## *Juniperus virginiana*, eastern red cedar.

If your horse has a cough, try a brew made from boiling the berries

*Juniperus virginiana*, eastern red cedar (tree).

and leaves of red cedar, *Juniperus virginiana*. It is supposed to be very simple to get a horse to drink the stuff — just put the bitter medicine in a long-necked bottle, then put the bottle's neck partway in the horse's mouth back of its teeth at the side, letting the liquid slowly run down its throat, holding its head up firmly all the while. The red cedar tea was prescribed for humans, too, so if you have a cough at the same time your horse has one, just share the medicine.

The eastern red cedar was a sacred tree to the Indians, so sacred that Sioux tribes up and down the Missouri River put red cedar poles on their tepees to ward off the lightning that flashed on the plains. Those who have lived on the wide grasslands of the Great Plains and had a lightning storm crackle in their ears can sympathize with the Indians' searching for anything that might help.

The Indians had a method of inhaling smoke that was foolproof.

*Juniperus virginiana*, eastern red cedar (needles).

They wrapped themselves loosely in a big blanket, and under the blanket they burned small twigs of the eastern red cedar (or whatever other plant was needed for a specific ailment) and inhaled the smoke that enveloped them as thickly as the blanket. Red cedar smoke was also held to be marvelous for curing a cold in the head.

If a member of the tribe was so nervous that he was having nightmares, back under the smoky blanket he went. The red cedar smoke would end the cold, the nervousness, and the bad dreams, and all would be well again.

Backwoodsmen in the eastern hills of America knew they could boil the tender leaves at the top of the tree to make a lavender dye. Others boiled those same leaves and drank the brew for the weakness that accompanied convalescence, to help them get well more quickly.

There might have been some real value in the red cedar leaves.

Recent developments find that the oil from the evergreen leaves has an ingredient needed in a counter-irritant ointment, a soothing ointment for skin problems.

With all that, the red cedar is still best known for its wood, which is wanted for lining cedar chests or closets. How many generations of young women have owned hope chests lined with cedar? How many cedar closets are built into homes today?

## *Larix laricina*, tamarack.

The tamarack is a tree that has several common names. You might know it as the eastern larch, American larch, black larch, red larch, or hackmatack, besides the better-known name of tamarack. Whatever it was called, the bark of this tree was steeped to cure distemper in a horse. The theory was that it would drive out inflammation and generate heat in the body.

Indians in the frontier lands of Wisconsin believed that theory completely; white settlers soon followed their lead in using the tamarack bark for a medicine and made a tincture or extract of the inner bark for chronic bronchitis, chronic inflammation of the urinary passages, and hemorrhages. Both whites and Indians made a poultice from the fresh bark.

The Ojibwa inhaled the smoke from a smudge prepared from the dried tamarack leaves or needles, which treated the same illnesses as the tea — bronchitis, urinary inflammations, and hemorrhages.

Tamarack roots were gathered by Ojibwa women and made into a tough thread for sewing parts of canoes together. Bags made from those root fibers were very durable, too. The tamarack was a valued tree from tip to root.

Tamarack likes boggy ground, and once started it matures to a clean, straight tree. Its inch-long blue-green needles look like those of evergreens, but they are deciduous, falling from the tree each fall and growing anew in the spring. Small tan cones add to the beauty of the tree.

## *Larrea divaricata*, spreading creosote bush.

## *Larrea tridentata*, Coville creosote bush.

A general description of these plants is in Chapter 9, "Arrows."

The creosote bushes were included in several medicinal recipes by the Indians of the southwestern desert areas. Of primary interest were the small thick evergreen leaves. Boiled to a mush, they were then

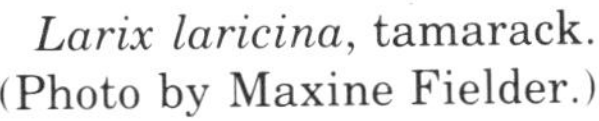

*Larix laricina*, tamarack.
(Photo by Maxine Fielder.)

*Osmorhiza longistylus*,
longstyle sweetroot or sweet cicely.

spread as a poultice on saddle sores that appeared on the Indians' horses.

The poultice would work just as well on wounds or burns suffered by the men or women themselves.

## *Osmorhiza longistylus*, longstyle sweetroot or sweet cicely.

A fourth distemper medicine was the longstyle sweetroot or smooth sweet cicely; in this case the root was needed. Fed to the beast, it would not only remedy the distemper but make the horse run faster as its condition improved.

The longstyle sweetroot was a very popular plant in frontier days with both Indians and white settlers. Sioux Indians pounded the root to make a poultice for boils or wounds. Meskwaki Indians in the northern part of the Midwest thought it was a good medicine for an eye infection, for the pangs of childbirth, and sore throat. Someone who was in puny health could mix sweet cicely leaves with the bark of *Gleditsia triacanthos*, honey locust, and soon he would be feeling fine again, regaining both his weight and his strength.

The sweet cicely root has a taste like licorice and is quite edible, but therein lies a danger. The sweet cicely looks a lot like poison hemlock, though it does not grow as tall as the poison hemlock.

The dull white flower umbels of the sweet cicely bloom at the top of stems sixteen to thirty-four inches high. You can smell the licorice odor on the sweet cicely root, but the poison hemlock has a bad smell, a really nauseous odor. The downy leaves of the sweet cicely are oval, but are pointed on the tips and strongly toothed along the edges.

The longstyle sweetroot has several popular names, including smooth sweet cicely, sweet myrrh, sweet anise, and western anise root.

## *Silphium laciniatum*, compass plant.

If a horse had worms, it was treated with a root decoction made from the compass plant, *Silphium laciniatum*, a wildflower that had a number of interesting virtues.

For humans, the root tea was valued not only as a tonic but, if the smaller roots were boiled, cooled, and drunk, as a good emetic. Naturally, because of the horse's larger intestinal tract, a stronger brew would have been concocted for it.

If the primitive American Indians did not have access to red cedar

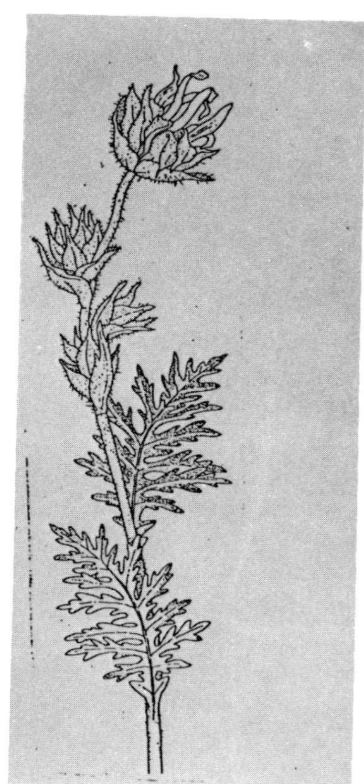

*Silphium laciniatum*, compass plant. (Drawing by Juan C. Barberis from *Plant Medicine and Folklore*, by Mildred Fielder, copyright 1975. Used by permission of Winchester Press.)

to protect them from lightning, they may well have burned the dried root of the compass plant, which grows from Michigan west and south. The compass plant was believed to be just as powerful for the job, and the Indians of the Missouri River region gathered it for protection against lightning.

This flower of the plains grows from five to ten feet high and has a rough, hairy texture and resinous sap. The yellow flowers are three to four inches in diameter and resemble a big sunflower except that the yellow rays of the blossoms are notched at the tips.

It gets its name compass plant from the alternate leaves, which tend to stand on edge and point northward and southward.

Little Indian children chewed the resinous stems like chewing gum, but the principal value of the plant lay in its roots.

White frontiersmen drank the root brew for rheumatism and for swollen glands when they had nothing better to take.

Other names for the compass plant include pilot weed and compass weed, both of these because of its directional tendencies, and gum weed or rosin weed for the resinous quality of the stems.

## *Zanthoxylum americanum*, common prickly ash.

The Pawnee Indians picked the fruits of the shrub, *Zanthoxylum americanum*, common prickly ash, to make a medicine for horses when the beasts were suffering from urine retention. The Sioux of the Missouri River basin also used the prickly ash fruits for a horse medicine that may have tackled the same problem, although I can find no mention of what kind of equine ailment they were supposed to treat.

Actually, the prickly ash berries, root bark, inner bark, trunk bark, and leaves were all cherished as extremely valuable medicine for humans as well, treating a variety of illnesses. What's good for the master certainly should be good for the horse.

I can't say what the Indian names of the prickly ash were, but white settlers knew it as the northern prickly ash, toothache tree, toothache bush, yellowwood, angelica tree, pellitory bark, or suterberry.

It is a small tree or shrub, generally growing from ten to twelve feet high. The branches have brown cone-shaped prickles (which give it one of its names) with five to eleven leaflets from one and a half to two inches long. Greenish yellow flowers bloom in the spring before the leaves appear. The bark and leaves have a good scent about them if you take time to sniff them closely.

The Omaha Indians gathered the fruits of the shrub and placed them among their clothing to perfume the garments.

Indian tribes in the Wisconsin forest considered everything on the

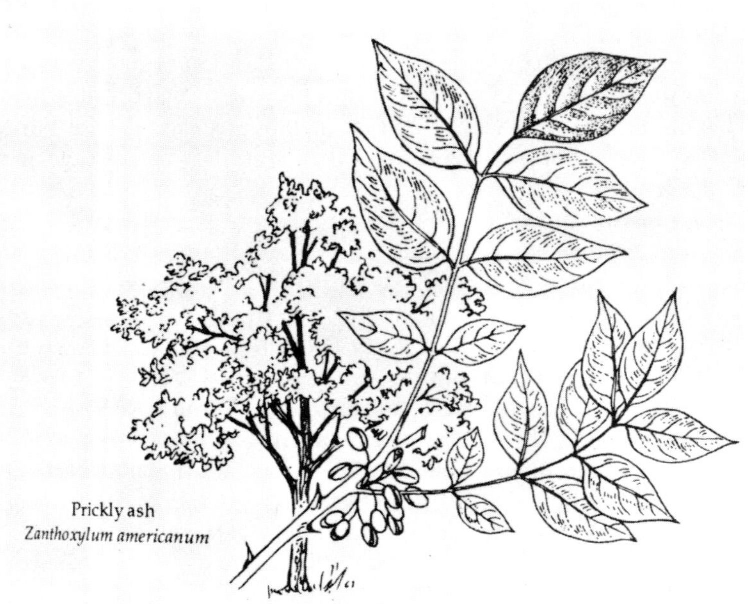


*Zanthoxylum americanum*, common prickly ash. (Drawing by Juan C. Barberis from *Plant Medicine and Folklore*, by Mildred Fielder, copyright 1975. Used by permission of Winchester Press.)

bush to be a medicine . They simmered the ripe berries in hot water and sprayed the brew on the chest or throat for bronchial diseases or sores. They made a poultice of the root bark for swellings. They drank the berry brew for minor maladies such as a sore throat, and added the bark to make a cough medicine and to treat hemorrhages and tuberculosis. They powdered the inner bark for a toothache remedy.

The Ojibwa, Meskwaki, and Menomini tribes all considered the prickly ash a sovereign remedy, and as time went by the white settlers seemed to agree with them.

The pioneers used prickly ash medicine as a stimulant and a diuretic, and to treat ailments of the pancreas, the liver, the kidneys, and the skin. It was also administered to promote sweating, and even to increase the pulse rate.

# EPILOGUE

# DOES THIS MAKE SENSE TODAY?

When you consider that commercial fish-bait enhancers are on the market today that contain the scent of berries or other fruits or herbs, these legendary wild-plant baits do indeed make sense.

Commercial fish lures use citrus oil effectively in many of the baits, because citrus oil helps to kill or mask human scent, whether the oil is in a liquid fish attractor or an animal lure. Even hand deodorants for hunters and fishermen are made with a citrus-oil base to keep human scent from the lures.

One of the fish baits manufactured today comes in several flavors — grape, blackberry, other fruit. Anise-seed elixir has always been a popular ingredient in commercial lures, which take its use beyond the simpler rubbing of the seeds on one's hands and bait.

As for enticing deer with apples, some commercial scents available in the sports shops today contain apples. The hunter using the apple lures is advised to sprinkle a few drops on game trails or areas frequented by browsing deer. In discussing this, veteran hunter Bob Elman notes:

> Some hunters hang up a small lure-impregnated bag like the little tobacco bag once popular among smokers who rolled their own. A small plastic bottle such as a vitamin-tablet bottle can be used this way; the bottle is filled with cotton impregnated with the lure. If the bag or bottle is set on a rock or log, or hung a foot or a foot and a half off the ground from a bush or sapling, the scent spreads more effectively on air currents. The hunter takes his stand within view and range of the lure. Interestingly, apple scent . . . will lure deer only in areas where the animals are used to browsing on the food involved. Where no wild or domestic apples grow, apple scent doesn't attract deer effectively.[1]

1. Robert Elman, personal letter to the author, July 18, 1980.

Other commercially prepared lures combine apple scent with glandular musk from the female deer. Bucks in rutting season really go for that one, quite naturally, and the idea is that if the apple smell is not enough to attract your buck, the doe musk wrecks his resistance.

In comparing the commercial baits to the wild plants that we have reported as legendary hunting and fishing aids, take a long look at the kinds of plants recommended in this book.

Many of the plants included in fish baits or hunting baits are edible by humans as well. The medical items known to help a horse in its illnesses are those equally well known for aiding mankind in various miseries.

Bows and arrows can be made from trees and shrubs scattered from coast to coast, bearing branches strong and pliant, rugged and durable for the strenuous sport of hunting and killing wild game.

Some of the insect repellents that have been acknowledged for centuries are still popular today, such as witch hazel, which you can buy in any drugstore as easily as you could a century or more ago. You can certainly make your own in the woods if you want to do so, but a finer product is available at the drugstore if you want it.

Garden herbs have found their way into the legends of hunting and fishing lures — flavoring, enticing, masking the human scent. One cannot afford to ignore them.

Mints, fruits, roots of various kinds, barks in the trees, sap from the woods. Granted not all of these wild plants are edible. Consider the ones described in Chapter 13, "Fish Narcotics," or the bushman's poison, which is added to an arrow tip.

The main thing that must be remembered is that once upon a time hunters and fishermen had to rely on their skill as woodsmen to help them get meat for the hungry family waiting for them.

That knowledge can still be valuable today. Not only can it help you to hunt and fish more effectively; it can also help you to feel a kinship with the hunters and fishermen, red and white, who have gone before.

# BIBLIOGRAPHY


ANDERSON, BARRETT HICKS. *A Contribution to the Flora of Montana de Oro State Park, California.* With dried flower collection. Master's thesis, California Polytechnic State University, 1972.

ANDERSON, FRED. "Stalking the Wild Rice." *Northliner Magazine*, Fall 1971.

ANDERSON, RAYMONA M. "Bois d'Arc." *Oklahoma Today*, Fall 1975.

ANGIER, BRADFORD. *Field Guide to Edible Wild Plants.* Harrisburg, Pa.: Stackpole Books, 1974.

ARMSTRONG, MARGARET. *Field Book of Western Wild Flowers.* New York: G.P. Putnam, 1915.

ARMSTRONG, MOSES K. *The Early Empire Builders of the Great West.* 1866. Reprint. St. Paul: E.W. Porter, 1901.

ARNOLD, AUGUSTA FOOTE. *The Sea-Beach at Ebb-Tide: A Guide to the Study of the Seaweeds and the Lower Animal Life Found Between the Tide Marks.* 1901. Reprint. New York: Dover Publications, 1968.

ASHIN, DEBORAH. *The Herb in Antiquity: A Look into the J. Paul Getty Museum Herb Garden.* Los Angeles: The J. Paul Getty Museum, 1976.

ASHTON, RUTH E. *Plants of Rocky Mountain National Park.* Washington, D.C.: U.S. Government Printing Office, 1953.

AUSTIN, MARY. *The Flock.* Santa Fe: William Gannon, 1973.

BAKELESS, JOHN. *The Eyes of Discovery.* Philadelphia: J.B. Lippincott Co., 1950.

BALLS, EDWARD K. *Early Uses of California Plants.* Berkeley and Los Angeles: University of California Press, 1972.

BARR, CLAUDE. *Native Plants from the High Plains, Badlands and Black Hills.* South Dakota: privately printed, 1954.

"Black Hills Plants." *Black Hills Engineer*, May 1931.

BLAKE, WILLIAM. "My Silks and Fine Array." In *Poems of William Blake.* Edited by W.B. Yeats. London: George Routledge & Sons; New York: E.P. Dutton & Co. n.d.

BOY SCOUTS OF AMERICA. *Revised Handbook for Boys.* New York: National Supply Service of Boy Scouts of America, 1942.

BRACKENRIDGE, H.M. *Journal of a Voyage up the River Missouri, 1808*. 1816. Reprint. In *Early Western Travels*, edited by Reuben G. Thwaites. Cleveland: Arthur H. Clark Co., 1904.

BRADBURY, JOHN. *Travels in the Interior of America, 1809–1811*. 1819. Reprint. In *Early Western Travels*, edited by Reuben G. Thwaites. Cleveland: Arthur H. Clark Co., 1904.

BRANDSTADT, DR. WAYNE. "One Person Command Best." *Lead (S.D.) Daily Call*, August 1868.

BRECK, JOSEPH. *New Book of Flowers*. New York: Orange Judd and Co., 1866.

BRITTON, NATHANIEL LORD, and BROWN, HON. ADDISON. *Illustrated Flora of the Northern United States, Canada and the British Possessions*. New York: Charles Scribner's Sons, 1913.

BROCK, PAUL. "The Magic of Fire-Walking at Sri Lanka." *San Franciso Chronicle*, July 7, 1980.

BROCKMAN, C. FRANK. *Trees of North America*. New York: Golden Press, 1968.

BRUNKEN, PEARL. "Summer and Wine!" *Rapid City* (S.D.) *Journal*, May 20, 1973.

CAPPS, MARY NEELY. "The Versatile Yucca, Candles of the Lord." *Oklahoma Today*, Autumn 1972.

CHACE, EARL. "It Comes Naturally." *Rapid City (S.D.) Journal*, May 7, 1972.

CHITTENDEN, HIRAM MARTIN. *American Fur Trade of the Far West*. New York: Press of the Pioneers, 1935.

CLEMENTS, FREDERIC E., and CLEMENTS, EDITH S. *Rocky Mountain Flowers*. 1914. 3rd ed. New York: H.W. Wilson Co., 1945.

*Colliers Encyclopedia*. New York: P.F. Collier and Son, 1954.

COLLINS, BARBARA J. *Key to Coastal and Chaparral Flowering Plants of Southern California*. California State University Foundation, n.d.

*Conservation List, 1976*. California Garden Clubs, Inc., 1976.

"Cook Dandelion Greens." *Rapid City (S.D.) Journal*, May 31, 1964.

COUES, ELLIOTT. *Lewis and Clark Expedition 1804–1806*. Washington, D.C.: U.S. Army Corps of Engineers, 1968.

DANA, MRS. WILLIAM STARR. *How to Know the Wild Flowers*. New York: Scribner's, 1899.

DAYTON, WILLIAM A. *Notes on Western Range Forbs*. Washington, D.C.: Forest Service, U.S. Department of Agriculture, 1960.

DOUGLAS, ROSE. "Wild Sandhill Plums." *Oklahoma Today*, Autumn 1974.

"Dreams Still Guide Destiny of Millions." *Rapid City* (S.D.) *Daily Journal*, Oct. 14, 1962.

DREGER, E. VERNA. "Community Spirit Characterized South Dakota Homesteading Days." *Rapid City* (S.D.) *Daily Journal*, April 27, 1958.

"Dr. Nature." *The Organic Morning Glory Message*, July 1971.

*Encyclopedia Americana*. New York: Americana Corp., 1949.

*Encyclopedia Americana*. 1965 ed. New York: Americana Corp., 1965.

ESHLEMAN, ALAN M. "Eating Off the Land." *San Francisco Sunday Examiner and Chronicle*, Aug. 18, 1974.

FERNALD, M.L., ed. *Gray's Manual of Botany*. 8th ed. New York: American Book Co., 1950.

FIELDER, MILDRED. *Plant Medicine and Folklore*. Tulsa: Winchester Press, 1975.

FOREST SERVICE, U.S. DEPARTMENT OF AGRICULTURE. *Range Plant Handbook.* Washington, D.C.: U.S. Government Printing Office, 1937.

FOX, HELEN M. *The Years in My Herb Garden.* 1953. Reprint. New York: Macmillan, 1973.

GEARY, IDA. "Some Thoughts on Weeds." *San Francisco Chronicle,* March 30, 1980.

GIBBONS, EUELL. *Stalking the Wild Asparagus.* New York: McKay Co., 1962.

GILMORE, MELVIN R. *Indian Lore and Indian Gardens.* Ithaca: Slengerland-Comstock Co., 1930.

———. *Plant Relations in North Dakorta.* Grand Forks, N.D.: University of North Dakota, 1921.

———. *Uses of Plants by the Indians of the Missouri River Region,* Bureau of American Ethnology Report, 1911–1912. Washington, D.C.: U.S. Government Printing Office, 1919.

GLEASON, HENRY A. *The New Britton and Brown Illustrated Flora of the United States and Canada.* Lancaster, Pa.: Lancaster Press, 1952.

GOTTSCHO, SAMUEL. *Pocket Guide to the Wildflowers.* New York: Pocket Books, 1951.

GRAY, ASA. *Botany of the Northern United States.* 1889

———. *New Manual of Botany.* 7th ed. New York: American Book Co., 1908.

———. *School and Field Book of Botany.* New York: Ivison, Blakeman, Taylor and Co., 1873.

GREENE, H.C., AND CURTIS, J.T. *A Bibliography of Wisconsin Vegetation.* Milwaukee: Milwaukee Public Museum, 1955.

*Guide to the Garden.* Santa Barbara: Santa Barbara Botanic Garden, n.d.

HAMMOCK, MARIE P. "Gardening, Why Not Follow Your Nose?" *San Francisco Examiner and Chronicle,* Feb. 29, 1976.

HANSEN, HARRY, ed. *The World Almanac and Book of Facts,* 1960. New York: New York World-Telegram and the Sun, 1960.

HARRINGTON, H.D. *Manual of the Plants of Colorado.* Denver: Sage Books, 1954.

HAWK, JOY KEVE. "Spouting Off." *Rapid City* (S.D.) *Journal,* April 22, 1962.

"Herb for Abortions Kills a Woman." *San Francisco Chronicle,* Dec. 2, 1978.

HERSEY, JEAN. "The Magic of Wild Flowers." *Woman's Day,* August 1965.

———. *The Woman's Day Book of Wildflowers.* New York: Simon & Schuster, 1960.

HIGGINS, ETHEL BAILEY. *Chaparral.* San Diego: San Diego Society of Natural History, n.d.

———. *Native Food Plants.* San Diego: San Diego Society of Natural History, 1952.

———. *Native Trees of San Diego County.* San Diego: San Diego Society of Natural History, 1952.

HOOVER, ROBERT. *Color Supplement to the Vascular Plants of San Luis Obispo County, California.* San Luis Obispo, Calif.: San Luis Obispo County Chapter of the California Native Plant Society, 1974.

HOUSE, HOMER D. *Wild Flowers.* New York: Macmillan, 1942.

IRVING, WASHINGTON. *Captain Bonneville.* New York: Collier, 1868.

"Jimson Weed is a Beautiful but Weird, Botanical Deceiver." *Lead* (S.D.) *Daily Call,* Oct. 24, 1960.

KELSEY, HARLAN, AND DAYTON, WILLIAM A. *Standardized Plant Names.* 2d ed. Prepared for the American Joint Committee on Horticultural Nomenclature. Harrisburg, Pa.: J. Horace McFarland Co., 1942.

KING, WAYNE. "Ginseng—the Root for All Reasons." *San Francisco Chronicle,* Oct. 26, 1975.

KIPPING, JOHN. "Dyeing With Plants." Mimeographed material used in connection with course titled "Indian Uses of Native Plants." University of California, Berkeley, 1973.

______. "Indian Use Plants That May Be Seen in the California Native Section." Mimeographed material used in lecture course. University of California, Berkeley, 1973.

KIPPING, JOHN, AND KIPPING, KATHERINE. Mimeographed material used in connection with course titled "Indian Uses of Native Plants." University of California, Berkeley, 1973.

KIRK, DONALD R. *Wild Edible Plants of Western North America.* Healdsburg, Calif.: Naturegraph Publishers, 1970.

KOHMAN, EDWARD F. "The Chemical Components of Onion Vapors Responsible for Wound Healing Qualities." *Science Magazine,* Dec. 26, 1947.

LARPENTEUR, CHARLES. *Forty Years a Fur Trader.* New York: Harper, 1898.

LAWHON, JEAN. "Springtime's Hidden Treasure." *The P.E.O. Record,* April 1975.

LEE COUNTY COLUMBIAN CLUB. *Recollections of the Pioneers of Lee County.* Dixon, Ill.: Inez A. Kennedy, 1893.

LEGG, KEN. *Point Lobos Wildflowers.* Department of Parks and Recreation, State of California, 1954.

LENZ, LEE W. *Native Plants for California Gardens.* 1956. Reprint. Claremont, Calif.: Rancho Santa Ana Botanic Garden, 1973.

LEWIS, MERIWETHER, AND CLARK, WILLIAM. *Original Journals of the Lewis and Clark Expedition.* Edited by Reuben G. Thwaites. New York: Dodd, Mead & Co., 1904.

LINDBERG, INGRID. "Here's How to Salt Those Home Grown Sunflower Seeds." *Rapid City* (S.D.) *Journal,* Oct. 14, 1973.

"Lustful Drugs for Listless People." *San Francisco Chronicle,* July 30, 1977.

MACINTOSH, ARTHUR C. *A Botanical Survey of the Black Hills of South Dakota.* Rapid City, S.D.: South Dakota State School of Mines, May 1931.

MATTHEWS, F. SCHUYLER. *Field Book of American Wild Flowers.* New York: G.P. Putnam, 1927.

MAXIMILIAN, PRINCE OF WIED. *Travels in the Interior of North America.* In *Early Western Travels,* edited by Reuben G. Thwaites. Cleveland: Arthur H. Clark Co., 1906.

McCABE, CHARLES. "Garlic and Love." *San Francisco Chronicle,* Nov. 22, 1974.

McDOUGALL, W.B., AND BAGGLEY, HERMA A. *Plants of Yellowstone National Park.* Washington, D.C.: U.S. Government Printing Office, 1936.

MEDSGER, OLIVER PERRY. *Edible Wild Plants.* New York: Macmillan, 1939.

MEYER, JOSEPH E. *The Herbalist.* Hammond, Ind.: Hammond Book Co., 1934.

MILORADOVICH, MILO. *The Home Garden Book of Herbs and Spices.* Garden City, N.Y.: Doubleday, 1952.

*Modern American Encyclopedia*. New York: Instructive Books, 1949.

MOLNER, DR. JOSEPH G. Column in *Rapid City* (S.D.) *Journal*, Feb. 7, 1964.

MUENSCHER, WALTER C. *Poisonous Plants of the United States*. New York: Macmillan, 1939.

MUNZ, PHILIP A. *California Desert Wildflowers*. Berkeley and Los Angeles: University of California Press, 1962.

———. *California Spring Wildflowers: From the Base of the Sierra Nevada and Southern Mountains to the Sea*. Berkeley and Los Angeles: University of California Press, 1961.

NATIONAL GEOGRAPHIC SOCIETY. *The Book of Wild Flowers*. Washington, D.C.: National Geographic Society, 1924.

THE NATURE CONSERVANCY. "Desert Tortoise Shares a Ride to a Cultural History Lesson." *Golden Gardens*, Journal of the California Garden Clubs, Inc., Long Beach, Calif., July-August 1979.

NELSON, RUTH ASHTON. *Plants of Rocky Mountain National Park*. Washington, D.C.: U.S. Government Printing Office, 1953.

*New Pronouncing Dictionary of Plant Names*. 6th ed. Chicago: Florists Publishing Co., 1948.

NOVAK, F.A. *The Pictorial Encyclopedia of Plants and Flowers*. Edited by J.G. Barton. New York: Crown Publishers, 1966.

NUTTALL, THOMAS. *Journal of Travels into the Arkansas Territory*. 1821. Reprint. In *Early Western Travels*, edited by Reuben G. Thwaites. Cleveland: Arthur H. Clark Co., 1905.

ODDO, SANDRA. "How to get a Kick out of Dandelions." *House & Garden*, May 1974.

ORR, ROBERT T., AND ORR, MARGARET C. *Wild Flowers of Western America*. New York: Alfred A. Knopf, 1974.

OVER, WILLIAM H. *Flora of South Dakota*. Vermillion, S.D.: University of South Dakota, 1932.

OVER, WILLIAM H., and CHURCHILL, EDWARD P. *Mammals of South Dakota*. Vermillion, S.D.: University of South Dakota, 1945.

PADEN, IRENE D., and SCHLICHTMANN, MARGARET E. *The Big Oak Flat Road*, pp. 161–62. Yosemite National Park: Yosemite Natural History Association, 1959.

PARSONS, MARY ELIZABETH. *The Wild Flowers of California*. 5th ed. San Francisco: California Academy of Sciences, 1955.

PESMAN, M. WALTER. *Meet the Natives*. Denver: Smith Brooks, 1946.

PETRY, E.J. *Weeds and Their Control*. Bulletin No. 211. Brookings, S.D.: South Dakota State College Experiment Station, December 1924.

"Plants." *Black Hills Engineer*, January 1930.

PLATT, RUTHERFORD. *A Pocket Guide to the Trees*. New York: Pocket Books 1952.

"Poison in the Back Yard." *Family Safety*, Summer 1964.

*Poisonous Plants of Southern California*. Arcadia, Calif.: County of Los Angeles, Department of Arboreta and Botanic Gardens, n.d.

POLLACK, PENNY. "San Luis Obispo County's Harvest of Wild Foods." *Central*

*Coast Times* (San Luis Obispo, Calif.), June 24, 1976.

PRESTON, RICHARD J. *Rocky Mountain Trees*. Ames: Iowa State College Press, 1947.

PUCKETT, EDITH. "Let's Go Native!" *Golden Gardens*, November-December, 1978.

RANDOLPH, VANCE. *Ozark Mountain Folks*. New York: Vanguard Press, 1932.

REBBECK, DICK. "Survival Definite Possibility if You Rely on Native Hills Plants." *Rapid City* (S.D.) *Daily Journal*, Aug. 17, 1960.

REMINGTON, JOSEPH P., assisted by COOK, E. FULLERTON. *The Practice of Pharmacy*. 6th ed. Philadelphia: J.B. Lippincott Co., 1917.

RICE, WILLIAM. "Some Eat Garlic, Some Don't." *San Francisco Chronicle*, April 19, 1975.

RICKETT, H.W., ed. *Wild Flowers of America*. New York: Crown Publishers, 1953.

ROBBINS, W.W.; BELLUE, MARGARET K.; and BALL, WALTER S. *Weeds of California*. Sacramento: Documents and Publications, State of California, 1970.

ROBERTS, HAROLD, and ROBERTS, RHODA. *Colorado Wild Flowers*. Denver: Bradford-Robinson Printing Co., 1959.

RUSSELL, J. ALMUS. "Doctoring with Herbs." *Frontiers Magazine*, February 1957.

RYDBERG, P.A. *Flora of the Rocky Mountains and Adjacent Plains*. New York: privately printed, 1917.

SARGENT, CHARLES SPRAGUE. *Manual of the Trees of North America*. Boston and New York: Houghton Mifflin Co., 1905.

SAUNDERS, CHARLES FRANCIS. *Useful Wild Plants of the United States and Canada*. New York: Robert M. McBride Co., 1920.

———. *Western Flower Guide: Wild Flowers of the Rockies and West to the Pacific*. 1917. Reprint. Garden City, N.Y.: Doubleday, Page and Co., 1923.

SHARPE, GRANT, and SHARPE, WENONAH. *101 Wildflowers of Crater Lake National Park*. Seattle: University of Washington Press, 1959.

———. *101 Wildflowers of Mt. Ranier National Park*. Seattle: University of Washington Press, 1957.

———. *101 Wildflowers of Olympic National Park*. Seattle: University of Washington Press, 1957.

———. *101 Wildflowers of Shenandoah National Park*. Seattle: University of Washington Press, 1958.

SHUMWAY, HERBERT D. *Nature Photography Guide*, 3d. ed. New York: Chilton Book Co., 1959.

SHUTE, NEVIL. *An Old Captivity*. New York: Lancer Books, 1962.

SIEVERS, A.F. *American Medicinal Plants of Commercial Importance*. Miscellaneous Publication No. 77. Washington, D.C.: U.S. Department of Agriculture, July 1930.

SMITH, HURON H. *Ethnobotany of the Menomini Indians*. Bulletin of the Public Museum of the City of Milwaukee, vol. 4, no. 1. Milwaukee: Public Museum of the City of Milwaukee, Dec. 10, 1923.

———. *Ethnobotany of the Meskwaki Indians*. Bulletin of the Public Museum of the City of Milwaukee, vol. 4, no. 2. Milwaukee: Public Museum of the City of Milwaukee, April 7, 1928.

———. *Ethnobotany of the Ojibwe Indians*. Bulletin of the Public Museum of the City of Milwaukee, vol. 4, no. 3. Milwaukee: Public Museum of the City of Milwaukee, May 2, 1932.

"Spikes of Cattails Called a Delicacy." *Rapid City* (S.D.) *Daily Journal*, July 3, 1960.

STANDLEY, PAUL C. *Plants of Glacier National Park*. Washington, D.C.: U.S. Government Printing Office, 1926.

SWARTZLOW, CARL R., AND UPTON, ROBERT F. *Badlands National Monument, South Dakota*. Natural History Handbook Series No. 2. Washington, D.C.: U.S. Government Printing Office, 1957.

TAYLOR, NORMAN. *A Guide to the Wild Flowers*. Garden City, N.Y.: Garden City Publishing Co., 1928.

THAYER, WALT. Letter to the editor. *Old West*, Fall 1969.

THOSTESON, DR. G.C. "Ask the Doctor." *San Francisco Chronicle*, Nov. 22, 1974.

THWAITES, REUBEN G., ed. *Early Western Travels*. Cleveland: Arthur H. Clark Co., 1904, 1905, 1906.

"Tiny Ragweed Pollen Creates Major Misery." *Rapid City* (S.D.) *Daily Journal*, Aug. 31, 1960.

TOWNSEND, JOHN K. *Narrative of a Journey Across the Rocky Mountains*. 1839. Reprint. In *Early Western Travels*, edited by Reuben G. Thwaites. Cleveland: Arthur H. Clark Co., 1905.

TRESIDDER, MARY CURRY, and HOSS, DELLA TAYLOR. *The Trees of Yosemite*. 1932. Rev. ed. Stanford: Stanford University Press, 1948.

"Uses Found for Common Cattail." *Rapid City* (S.D.) *Daily Journal*, June 9, 1954.

"Using Those Weeds, Plantain." *The Organic Morning Glory Message*, July 1971.

VAN BRUGGEN, THEODORE. *Wildflowers of the Northern Plains and Black Hills*. Badlands Natural History Association Bulletin No. 3. Interior, S.D.: National Park Service, U.S. Department of the Interior, 1971.

VERNAM, GLENN R. *The Rawhide Years*. Garden City, N.Y.: Doubleday & Co., 1976.

*The Volume Library*. New York: Educational Publishers, 1939.

WATSON, LLOYD. "The S.F. Ginseng Tycoon, An Herb That Grew." *San Francisco Chronicle*, July 9, 1976.

WEBER, WILLIAM A. *Handbook of Plants of the Colorado Front Range*. Boulder: University of Colorado Press, 1961.

WEDGE, LUCILLE. "Famed Biblical Tree Favored in This Area," *Rapid City* (S.D.) *Journal*, Nov. 2, 1965.

WEEKLEY, ERNEST. *An Etymological Dictionary of Modern English*. New York: Dover Publications, 1967.

WELLS, VIRGINIA L. "Photographing Northern Wild Flowers." *The National Geographic Magazine*, June 1956.

WHERRY, EDGAR T. *Wild Flower Guide*. Garden City, N.Y.: Doubleday, 1948.

"Wild Salads and Wild Vegetables." *Sunset Magazine*, May 1976.

WRIGHT, MURIEL H. *American Indian Corn Dishes*. The Chronicles of Oklahoma, vol. XXXVI, no. 2. Oklahoma Historical Society.

ZIM, HERBERT S. *The Southeast*. New York: Golden Press, 1959.

ZIM, HERBERT S., AND MARTIN, ALEXANDER C. *Flowers: A Guide to Familiar American Wildflowers*. New York: Simon and Schuster, 1950.

———. *Trees: A Guide to Familiar American Trees*. New York: Simon and Schuster, 1956.

# INDEX OF COMMON NAMES